# Small Districts
# Big Problems

# Small Districts
# Big Problems

## *Making School Everybody's House*

Richard A. Schmuck
Patricia A. Schmuck

CORWIN PRESS, INC.
A Sage Publications Company
Newbury Park, California

*For information address*:

Corwin Press, Inc.
A Sage Publications Company
2455 Teller Road
Newbury Park, California 91320

SAGE Publications Ltd.
6 Bonhill Street
London EC2A 4PU
United Kingdom

SAGE Publications India Pvt. Ltd.
M-32 Market
Greater Kailash I
New Delhi 110 048 India

Printed in the United States of America

**Library of Congress Cataloging-in-Publication Data**

Schmuck, Richard A.
    Small districts, big problems: making school everybody's house /
Richard A. Schmuck, Patricia A. Schmuck.
        p.    cm.
    Includes bibliographical references and index.
    ISBN 0-8039-6025-5.—ISBN 0-8039-6026-3 (pbk.)
        1. School districts—United States—Case studies.    2. Cities and
towns—United States—Case studies.    I. Schmuck, Patricia A.
II. Title.
LB2817.3.S36    1992                                                          92-12420
379.1'535'0973—dc20                                                              CIP

92   93   94   95   10   9   8   7   6   5   4   3   2   1

Corwin Press Production Editor:  Tara S. Mead

# Contents

# Foreword

Richard and Patricia Schmuck make a significant contribution to those of us working in rural education as they share their "blue highways" odyssey in *Small Districts, Big Problems.* In this work, two nationally and internationally recognized educators have captured life in nonurban schools in a way that can only come from a rich understanding of public education and sharp perceptions from seeing something for the first time. Because they had not worked extensively in small or rural schools, they came with a "new set of eyes." And what they saw forces those of us who have spent our professional lives in the field to reexamine our perceptions, our biases, and even our nostalgic views of what small schools and rural communities represent. One comes away from reading the book saying, "Yes, that's right. That is the way it is."

The professional and personal lives of the Schmucks have been devoted to living out and promoting democratic participation in both individual and organizational relationships. Their work as educators

has been concerned with how we can make institutions more humane. Humanity toward one another springs from knowing and being
known or, using the Schmucks' words, the "I-Thou transactions." As
public schools have become larger and more bureaucratic, the possibility of the existence of such relationships diminishes, the victim
of our concerns for organizational efficiency. Students as well as
staff become depersonalized and redundant. Is it possible that there
might be relationships between school size and the level of democratic participation? Is it possible that rural schools, because of the
community culture and smaller scale, might be different? The fact
that the Schmucks recognized that differences exist between rural
and urban schools is to be commended. The fact that they actually
acted on this recognition and conducted their research in small
school districts sets a precedent for other researchers to follow. One
can only hope that others will follow the blue highways into this too
often overlooked segment of U.S. public education.

As the title *Small Districts, Big Problems* suggests, all is not well in
small rural schools. The inadequacies of our public education system,
particularly as it functions in small rural communities, take shape in the
rich descriptions of the lives of students, teachers, principals, superintendents, and school boards. The pervasiveness of the one-best-system,
factory model of education is inescapable. Constrained by the public
school infrastructure, the rules, the regulations, the categorical programs, rural schools have no choice but to operate like big schools.
Unfortunately, because they are smaller, they can never perform quite
as well as their larger counterparts. Historically, they have always been
considered "second best." Because the expectation is that small districts
should look and perform as much like large districts as they can, it is
not surprising that the Schmucks found the same undemocratic practices
in small schools. With the professionalization and specialization of
public education, even rural schools have embraced the characteristics
of urban institutions rather than the more familial relationships that are
more consistent with small, rural social structures. As one moves along
the blue highways with the Schmucks, one shares their disappointment
that they do not find more examples in which those who work and live
in rural schools take advantage of the small size and personal relationships to create a more humane approach to learning. Teachers, for

the most part, work in isolation. Instruction is still largely teachers in the front of the class talking and students listening passively. Administrators tend to be as distant from the teaching staff as they are in the larger settings.

*Small Districts, Big Problems* could not, however, have been written at a better time. The industrial model of schooling is increasingly coming under scrutiny for its shortcomings. Rising expectations for education, calls for school reform, and tighter budgets have created a situation where rural schools are increasingly under siege. The time is right for the emergence of "break the mold" approaches to schooling. The Schmucks, throughout the book, provide the beginnings of a road map to help rural schools and communities begin their own journey on the road to better schools. Sections in the book titled "Targets of Change" provide guidance on what can be done differently in the classroom, how staff meetings can be conducted so they are more effective, and how links to the community can be strengthened.

*Small Districts, Big Problems: Making School Everybody's House* is a book that has something to say to a diverse audience. Teachers, administrators, and school board members will find it a mirror to help them reflect on what they do and how they might do it better. Students training to become teachers in small communities will find it helpful in understanding the context within which they will work. Community members will see themselves and their potential contributions in its pages. There is a growing recognition that learning is lifelong, that what we need to strive for is the creation of learning communities. Nonurban communities, because of their size, could much more easily move in this direction than those in urban areas. It is indeed within the realm of possibility that the rural school could become everybody's house.

I invite you to travel with Patricia and Richard on their journey, following the blue highways to the small schools and rural communities of the land. Share in their stories of the physical and educational landscape. Their story represents research that connects with reality. It is writing that has heart and soul and therefore helps us all.

—*Paul Nachtigal*
Director, Rural Institute,
Mid-Continent Regional Educational Laboratory

# Preface

The two of us are modern examples of what Tocqueville described 150 years ago as restless Americans. Indeed, we have been smitten with what Steinbeck in *Travels With Charlie* called "the virus of restlessness." We have traveled to two and a half corners of the globe: Australia, China, Finland, Guam, Israel, and Russia. We spent a year in Belgium, where several times we kidnapped our two children from their Flemish Catholic schools to explore Denmark, France, Germany, Italy, Liechtenstein, Luxembourg, the Netherlands, Norway, and Sweden.

Most of our foreign travel has been to consult, lecture, collect data, or promote a book, and thus it has afforded a connection to foreign colleagues who have typically given us their personal views of their country and of ours. We have carefully avoided commercial tours and popular tourist sites. As we were struggling to find our way out of a thickly wooded hillside near Vianden, Luxembourg, where Victor

Hugo spent three summers writing *Les Misérables,* our son, Allen, at 13 years old, asked, "Can't we go anywhere where everyone else goes?" Allen was certain we would get lost and stumble into Germany, never again to find our passports, rented car, and personal belongings.

For those readers who love to travel, our journey will require little explanation. Avid travelers like us devour books by Paul Theroux, Charles Kuralt, and Bill Bryson; keep *Michelin Guides* at their bedsides; buy travel books for each other for Christmas; collect maps that never get framed; always choose *Arizona Highways* or *Southern Living* to read at the doctor's office; and never throw away *National Geographic.* If you fit our category, you will need no explanation for this study. If you are not a travel buff, however, let us explain.

As professionals, both of us are committed students of teaching and learning in formal educational settings. Our love affair with public schooling has gone on for our entire lives. We have been public school students, teachers, and administrators, professors of education, educational researchers and consultants, authors of educational texts, college and university administrators, and concerned parents active in our children's public schools. Although we have studied schools in most of the 50 states and Canada, we had not, until now, spent much time in rural and small-town schools. Most of our consulting, teaching, and research on schools has, heretofore, focused on schools in cities and suburbs.

To combine our penchant for travel with our love of schools and lack of experience with out-of-the-way places in America, we took to what William Least Heat Moon called the "blue highways" of America. We drove two-lane roads to visit 25 school districts in 21 states, traveling almost 10,000 miles in six months. We spent one week studying each of the small districts. We carried out this study on our sabbatical leaves from the University of Oregon and Lewis and Clark College during the winter and spring of 1989.

On an episode of *All in the Family,* Archie Bunker, a prototypical American redneck, defined a *sabbatical* as nothing more than a long vacation with pay. We aim to prove Archie wrong with this book. We have prepared it for a variety of readers, including classroom teachers, school administrators, board members, professors of education, and educational administrators and specialists in county offices and state departments of education. Although it will be of most interest to educators and citizens committed to small districts and small schools, we think that it also will interest educators and policymakers everywhere who strive to do the best job possible for America's young people.

We are grateful to the many educators and community residents who received us so warmly. The small-town people we met were friendly and gracious. We felt a genuine part of rural school life as we parked our RV on school parking lots and ate breakfast or lunch with friendly students. In addition to giving us time for formal interviews and observations, we also enjoyed relaxed, informal meetings with many generous educators. We were, for example, welcomed to a family birthday party for a young superintendent in Arizona. Also in Arizona, we enjoyed a magnificent collection of early Hohokam pottery and baskets in the home of a school board member. In Texas, we shared the joy of antique collecting with an elementary principal. In Arkansas, Illinois, and Montana, we were taken to dinner by superintendents, and, in a host of other places, we were given guided tours of local surroundings by principals or teachers. We still correspond with a superintendent in California and a teacher in Missouri. Although we cannot name the people with whom we conducted interviews for reasons of anonymity, we are appreciative and grateful for the assistance they gave us. We also thank Jerry McGuire, Ellie Perry, and Phil Runkel for their constructive criticism of earlier drafts of the manuscript.

We hope that you, the reader, will find our descriptive information to be brutally honest, even embarrassingly realistic, and our prescriptive recommendations to be intellectually inspirational, even morally uplifting. We believe not only that our research results are valid but also that our dream of making school everybody's house is an American archetype, a way of thinking about education grounded in the one-room, rural schoolhouse and reechoed throughout the history of the American experiment in democracy.

*Richard A. Schmuck*
University of Oregon
*Patricia A. Schmuck*
Lewis and Clark College

# About the Authors

*Small Districts, Big Problems: Making School Everybody's House* is the third book the Schmucks have coauthored. Their previous books were *Group Processes in the Classroom* (1992, William C. Brown, now in its 6th edition and translated into Hebrew, Spanish, and Norwegian) and *A Humanistic Psychology of Education* (1974, Mayfield). The Schmucks have been working in public education for more than 30 years as authors, teachers, researchers, and consultants. They have also contributed to public schools as parents and citizens: For example, they helped create Eastside Public Alternative School in 1973, which still exists in Eugene, Oregon, where their currently adult children, Julie and Allen, spent some of their formative years.

Richard is an action-oriented social psychologist of education. Patricia, a former public school teacher and administrator, focuses on gender roles in education and leadership training for school administrators. Both are graduates of the University of Michigan:

Richard was an English major and Phi Beta Kappa, and Patricia was an elementary education major with a master's in special education. Richard earned his Ph.D. in social psychology from the University of Michigan, focusing on the influence of peers in the classroom. He worked under the tutelage of Ronald Lippitt, whose dissertation with Kurt Lewin on the effects of autocratic, democratic, and laissez-faire leadership in children's groups has become a classic. Patricia earned her Ph.D. from the University of Oregon, conducting one of the first studies on women as school administrators.

After leaving the University of Michigan, the Schmucks lived in Philadelphia. Richard taught group dynamics and educational leadership at Temple University and worked on social problems of urban schools. Patricia taught at Wordsworth Academy, a private school for students with learning disabilities. They moved to Oregon in 1967, where Richard has been a Professor of Educational Psychology and Educational Administration at the University of Oregon. From 1976 to 1980, Patricia directed the Sex Equity and Educational Leadership Project at the University of Oregon; then, in 1981, she joined the faculty of Lewis and Clark College to develop the new program in educational administration, which she now directs.

Richard is nationally and internationally known for his work in organization development in schools. He is coauthor, with Phil Runkel, of *The Third Handbook of Organization Development in Schools*. With Runkel, he also was corecipient of the Douglas McGregor Memorial Award for outstanding research in applied behavioral science. He became the first President of the International Association for the Study of Cooperation in Education, founded in Tel Aviv, Israel. He is the author or coauthor of 15 books and more than 160 journal articles. Patricia has been a researcher and activist in gender issues; she is the coauthor of five books and numerous articles about women educators, including *Women Educators: Employees of Schools in Western Countries*. She also was a founder of Northwest Women in Educational Administration, an advocacy group for women school administrators.

The Schmucks have consulted and lectured in Australia, Belgium, China, Denmark, England, Finland, Germany, Guam, Israel, Italy, Mexico, the Netherlands, Norway, Portugal, Spain, and Sweden.

Prior to this study on small-town schools, their writing had focused on schools in the larger cities and crowded suburbs of California, Illinois, Michigan, New York, Pennsylvania, Oregon, and Washington.

Public schools are their vocation and avocation. Their sabbatical leave in 1989 combined their love of travel to out-of-the-way places and a study of schooling in small-town America. Their affinity for small towns and rural life is realized at their cottage in the Hood River Valley, where they grow apples and watch the changing colors of Mount Hood and where they plan to live in the next stage of their lives.

# 1

## The Troubled House Divided

> My town is boring
> because it doesn't have
> enough places to go.
> I'm too used to it.
> I could ride my bike through
> the whole town,
> like two blocks.
> Every time I ride my bike
> though,
> it gets smaller and smaller
> and smaller each time.
> —*Fourth grader*

Small districts continue to be an important component of the public schools in the United States. They exist in significant numbers in virtually all states. In New York, for example, out of the total of 723 K-12 districts, 245 (33%) serve fewer than 1,000 students. In Oregon too, one third of the 302 districts have fewer than 1,000 students, and half of those employ only one chief administrator, who functions in the dual capacity of superintendent and principal. Overall, small districts, defined as those having fewer than 3,000 students, constitute approximately 75% of districts in the nation and provide the schooling for about 30% of the elementary and secondary school-age population. And 51% of all districts are both small and rural. Although small districts still predominate, they are becoming fewer. In 1930, there were 128,000 districts nationwide and, after World War II, there were still more than 100,000, but today there are fewer than 16,000 school districts in the United States. During the last 60 years, the number of one-room elementary schools decreased from 150,000 to fewer than 1,000. As small districts have become fewer, attention has turned away from them; they are seldom studied and infrequently written about. It is the urban and suburban districts that get the attention of the researcher, the policymaker, and the press.

For us, however, small districts have a romantic allure. Their smallness offers the possibility of teachers giving individual attention to students and of administrators and teachers developing close, familylike ties between them. More than their urban counterparts, small districts have the feasibility of bringing administrators, parents, students, and teachers together in harmony to make school everybody's house.

## OUR VISITS TO SMALL DISTRICTS

To study both the assets and the problems of small districts, we spent six months driving almost 10,000 miles along what Least Heat Moon (1982) called the "blue highways" of America, those two-lane roads marked blue by the cartographer's pen. We visited 25 school districts off the beaten track and serving isolated incorporated towns in 21 states.

We went to find out about their accomplishments and their challenges in educating youngsters. We went also to find out about the problems and to discover how the small-district educators were grappling with them. We sought to collect information about especially effective practices, believing that smallness might facilitate school effectiveness.

In particular, we focused on districts serving small incorporated towns because we feared that small-town life could become a cultural anachronism in our lifetime and that the educational effectiveness of schools there would go unnoticed elsewhere. With the economic recession of the late 1980s, the continued mobility of citizens into urban areas, and the persistent social climbing in American society, we were concerned that the very heart of American culture—the small, secure community—would soon disappear. We wanted to study schools in small-town America before it was too late.

Using Dialog Information Services and a map, we randomly chose K-12 districts in incorporated towns that had 300 to 3,000 students and lay more than 75 miles from a college of education. We wanted to study districts that would not be inundated with university researchers and the supervisors of practice teachers. An introductory letter from Verne Duncan, then Oregon State Superintendent and Chief of the Chief State School Officers, and a letter from us explaining our purpose and proposed dates of our visit went to each selected district. Only one district refused our visit. Our actual sample of 25 districts ranged in size from 450 to 2,000 students, and the distances from teacher training sites, except for one private college with a small teacher training program, ranged from 75 to 250 miles. We visited districts serving students with ethnically mixed populations, many all white, one primarily Hispanic, one predominately black, and three districts serving Native American students living on reservations. We observed classes and meetings in 80 schools and interviewed a variety of superintendents, principals, board members, teachers, students, and a scattering of custodians, counselors, clergy, and citizens at large. We conducted group interviews of 19 classes and observed 50 more, from kindergarten to grade 12.

With optimism about the social-emotional benefits of small districts, we went searching for citizens participating in academic matters, administrators and teachers sharing influence and solving educational problems together, teachers collaborating about students' problems, students voicing their opinions about running the schools, and classrooms using cooperative learning and peer support. We went in search of schools different than the portrait of metropolitan schools painted by Goodlad (1984) as lacking collaboration and shared influence among administrators, parents, and teachers. After all, the classic literature on school and classroom size by Barker and Gump (1964) and Smith and Glass (1979) had indicated that smaller rather than larger units would manifest greater potential for collaborative relationships. Our guiding questions were these: Do small districts actualize collaboration and cooperation about academic matters better than the big urban and suburban districts? Are the administrators, teachers, and students less individuated and alienated in small districts? Are small, isolated districts more participatory than schools in dense population centers?

To paint our own portraits of small districts, we spent four days interviewing and observing in each district and the following two days of each week putting the data into a portable computer. The interviews were open-ended and semistructured. We started with general questions about the accomplishments and challenges of the district, funneling gradually toward specific questions and probes about interpersonal relationships and teaching and learning. We eventually asked everyone about his or her attitudes toward the interpersonal relationships in the district, school, and classroom. We merged notes, keeping for the computer only points about which we both agreed; overall, we amassed 750 single-spaced pages of notes on our portable (but reliable) Toshiba computer. In addition, we picked up statements on district philosophy and goals, board procedures, policy manuals, guidelines for student behavior, procedures to evaluate teachers, course syllabi, and newspaper clippings.

This book is not intended to review the literature on rural and small schools. For those interested in a comprehensive review of the literature, we refer you to the excellent review by Alan DeYoung (1987), the edited volumes of Jonathan Sher (1977, 1981), Paul Nachtigal (1982), and DeYoung (1991), the ethnographic studies of Alan Peshkin (1978, 1982), and the history of rural education by Wayne Fuller (1982).

## The Vulnerable Vortex

Rivers rush relentlessly out of the Cascade mountains of Central Oregon, bringing the snow to the sea. As "river rats," we delight in maneuvering our rubber rafts over the white rapids and waves to experience both an exhilarating ride and the joy of cooperative teamwork in a group of four to six. The wild, untamed river allows for a welcome lull now and then in the form of an eddy, a safe, whirling vortex of water with a vacuum at its center into which anything caught in its motion is drawn. The river's vortex can offer a resting place for the rafters before taking on the next challenge of the unforgiving river.

Descartes believed that vortexes of fluid could account for the very formation of the universe. Our experiences in small districts indicated that these districts are like a vortex, drawing everyone into them and serving as the foundation or heart of the community. The small school engages virtually everyone because, like the river's eddy, it irresistibly draws the community's residents into it. The small town, like the eddy, encompasses everything within its tenacious reach. The people in small towns surrender their privacy, independence, and autonomy. Instead of being anonymous, they seek relationships that they report are friendly, supportive, and caring. Administrators and teachers are public figures; they must be concerned with propriety and public relations, because the people's thoughts about their community center on the school. People go to the school for education, entertainment, social life, and community identity. In one town of 5,200, it was reported that the Christmas pageant draws 6,000 spectators (we note this was definitely a *Christmas* pageant; there was no euphemism of a "winter pageant"). Much more than the church, city hall, or tavern, the small school district occupies the townspeople for considerable time in its classes, sports events, club meetings, potluck dinners, recreational events, musical concerts, open houses, and theatrical presentations before they return again to the flow of private life.

Rock formations near the banks of Oregon rivers like the Deschutes, Rogue, and Umpqua are unstable. Under the upheaval of earthquakes and Pacific storms, fallen timber comes crashing into rocks, shooting them off like giant marbles into the river, changing the river's course, its flow, and its churning. Wise rafters realize that the river will be different from year to year. They must rediscover again and again the recently fallen boulders, the new white water, the location of logs, and the new location of the eddy. The safe vortex of a season ago could be the vulnerable and dangerous vortex of today.

The small-town school district is the vulnerable vortex of the 1990s. More than 75% of the towns we visited were in deep *economic trouble*. Those that were not poor were blessed with desirable scenery and recreational facilities for tourism, a military post, or a well-endowed private college. Many, however, were virtual ghost towns in which the number of stores had shrunk to 25% of the number 10 years before. Strategically placed shopping malls set out between small towns were draining shoppers from more than half of the places we went. Local newspapers were scraping to get by on sharply reduced advertising. In some of the towns, the schools were having problems attracting high-ability teachers, particularly in the sciences. In other small districts, experienced teachers of 10 to 12 years were being discharged because of budget reductions, and other districts hadn't hired a new teacher in many years. In all but those districts fortunate to receive federal impact funds, we saw superintendent after superintendent struggling with a tight budget.

Whether the town's economy was based on copper, cotton, cattle, or climate (as in the Southwest) or on grain, corn, and hogs (as in the Midwest), small-town districts were in severe economic jeopardy. Inequitable state funding, antiquated industries, and vanishing small farms were drastically changing the portrait of many small districts that had relied on a single economic source. As the economic conditions have worsened, teachers have remained the last and often the only professional class of workers in town. School board membership also reflected the economic changes, with fewer and fewer well-educated professionals serving.

Many of the former middle managers of industry and owners of small- and medium-sized farms had left, leaving a widening class disparity in many small-town districts. Teachers and administrators often remained the only bureaucratic workers in a struggling entrepreneurial economy. One town, still hurting from a teachers' strike, demonstrated the disparity between the bureaucratic teachers and the entrepreneurial community. The teachers were asking for an increase in medical and retirement benefits, but the board, unsympathetic with the teachers' wishes, was composed entirely of farmers and other entrepreneurs who had to pay for their own medical insurance and retirement. Where once small-town school districts embodied the family roots, today they attract more and more of the uprooted. Where once small towns were relatively stable, today they have a significant migratory population.

The increasing poverty of small-town America not only influences the norms of life in small towns, it changes the character of the students served by the small districts. Most teachers and principals we interviewed noted the rising population of emotionally and intellectually needy children served by today's school. Bane and Ellwood (1989) pointed out that 30% of children who fall below the poverty level live in rural communities, and the sobering demographic data of Hodgkinson (1986) indicated that the white and middle-class population, whom the schools have served most well in the past, are giving way to minority and lower-class population of students, whom the schools have served least well in the past.

## THE BIG PROBLEMS OF SMALL DISTRICTS

Although the economic circumstances of the small districts we visited were dire and ominous, the biggest problems were social-emotional. We were discouraged by the lack of interpersonal openness and the absence of mutual understanding we saw present in the relationships between students, teachers, and administrators. We did not find as much collaboration and cooperation in the classrooms and schools as we expected. Rarely did we find excitement and enthusiasm about teaching and learning. Instead, we found the following:

• Students were busy with extracurricular activities, but it was rare for students to tell us that they were enthusiastic about schoolwork. When we asked secondary students how they felt about classroom participation, again and again we heard the lilting refrain, "bor-ing!" Even though the typical school classes we observed had fewer than 20 students, we saw only a few cases of active discussion that drew in more than a couple of students and the teacher.

• Elected student leaders felt they had very little influence over school operations. We found no school in which the student council had a discernible effect on any aspect of school life, except social events. Although in two schools we did find formal surveys of students' attitudes toward school, in both places the purpose was to respond to a statewide mandate for school evaluation rather than a local initiative for school improvement.

• Formal collegial collaboration between teachers was occurring infrequently, despite the small size and presumed family spirit of the school. We saw only 3 out of 80 schools in which peer coaching and interdisciplinary teamwork were even being considered. Teachers were communicating informally with one another but (from what we heard) mostly to complain about parents, administrators, and students. The teachers were not meeting to solve academic problems or to make decisions about instruction.

• Administrators were much more likely than teachers to view their participation with teachers favorably. Formal meetings between principals and teachers were particularly ineffective in eliciting open and frank exchanges. Of the 80 schools we visited, only 10 principals had ways of enlisting teachers' feedback or had advisory committees of teachers that met regularly with the principals.

• Of the male administrators we met, 50% had been or still were coaches. Many of them saw communication and teamwork as unidirectional and hierarchical, as a sort of military teaming, rather than as transactional and egalitarian. In contrast, nine of the ten female principals we studied were more aware of the give-and-take of democratic reciprocity and skilled in it.

• In 80% of the classes, we observed what Flanders (1970) had labeled the "rule of two thirds": two thirds of classroom talk was teacher's talk, and two thirds of that was unidirectional lecturing. The high frequency of teacher talk was also reported more recently by Goodlad (1984). From our observations, we would modify Flanders's maxim to the "rule of three quarters" for small districts. That is shocking considering how small the classes were. And even more shocking, out of the 50 classes we observed, we saw only 3 instances of cooperative learning.

## THE SCHOOL AND COMMUNITY IDENTITY

The small-town school is the entertainment center of the community. Most citizens participate at some time in some events at the school. The high schools of small districts are particularly busy places. Many high school students arrive at school 30 minutes or more before classes begin and do not reach home until after 5:30 p.m. They participate in many extracurricular activities, including sports, music, theater, and service and special interest clubs. Approximately 40% of the teachers participate as coaches, sponsors, or advisers in after-school activities. The administrators spend as much time at school as the very busiest of students. On a Friday evening, two thirds of the town's population could be cheering on the boys at a football, basketball, or even hockey game, depending on the geographic location and the time of year. While girls had some sports available to them, in most towns it was the boys' sports that had a community following. The visiting-school team could have traveled by bus for as many as 175 miles in some rural areas and been followed by a caravan of 10 to 15 cars and minivans filled with fans.

In more than half of the small districts we visited, elementary and middle schools were used in the evenings for recreation, adult education, and community meetings. The elementary schools attracted more than 80% of parents and a large contingent of grandparents to open houses and evaluation conferences. There was no one in the towns we visited who didn't know where the schools were and, after we were in the district for a few days, it seemed there was no one in town who didn't know who we were. No matter whether we were in the West, South, Midwest, or Plains, citizens of all ages were being continually drawn into the town's safe eddy, its schools.

In fact, the culture of the small districts we visited extended beyond regional differences. A school in a Hispanic mining community of the Southwest, or one that was primarily black in the rich farmland of the Mississippi Delta, or a school built in 1893 and populated by the Norwegians of the Midwest all looked more alike than different. Horace Mann, perhaps the most influential educational policymaker of the nineteenth century, dreamed the school would unify, that it would serve the commonweal (see Cremin, 1951). Although some particular small district may not bring together diverse American subcultures, it always offers a common culture, regardless of where you go, for 5- to 18-year-olds in American society. And small districts, perhaps more than their large urban and suburban counterparts, do more than that; they bring citizens together to enhance a feeling of community identity.

If we had not carefully studied the interpersonal perceptions and feelings between students, teachers, and administrators, we could have easily concluded that the school of a small district is indeed everybody's house—a secure refuge in which citizens of any age can gather for personal growth and community development. But, even though the small-district high school, as the safe vortex of its community, offers the shelter and stage for public gatherings and community identity, it is a troubled house divided by its interpersonal closedness and misunderstandings. Rather than featuring what Buber (1958) called I-Thou relationships, too often small districts appear to be manifesting the I-It relationships of an impersonal, bureaucratic society.

## THE CASE FOR DEMOCRATIC PARTICIPATION

Buber taught that people learn how to be human through interpersonal meetings or encounters in which the participants communicate honestly and openly, sharing themselves with each other. Most interpersonal exchanges are of the I-It variety and do not consist of true "meeting." Role relationships are I-It; one person relates to another in terms of a category or function—storekeeper and shopper, conductor and passenger, teacher and student, administrator and teacher. I-Thou transactions are characterized instead by each person being recognized, appreciated, respected, and valued as a complete being. I-Thou transactions take place when "whole persons" encounter one another on an equal basis, each with full respect for the array of personal qualities to be found in the other.

We found that small districts, like their urban and suburban counterparts, fostered I-It transactions. Teachers thought mainly of their students' level of competence or motivation; they categorized them as "hard workers," "troublemakers," and "jocks," to mention a few. Even in elementary schools, where teachers can adopt a broader, more personal view, they usually categorized students within a subject matter perspective and judged them by their skills in mathematics, reading, social studies, art, or physical performance. While there is nothing wrong with such categories, their use does often put psychological distance between teachers and students. Similarly, administrator-teacher relationships also were primarily I-It transactions. The very organizational structures of the small districts kept students, teachers, and administrators isolated from one another both physically—in separated classrooms and isolated offices—and psychologically—through hierarchical decision making. Thus many of the small districts we visited were ruling out even the possibility of spontaneous I-Thou transactions by physically separating the participants and keeping them in status-role categories.

I-Thou transactions are most likely to take place in what sociologists refer to as "primary relationships," defined as characterized by egalitarianism, empathy, concern, and openness. We can also refer to such interpersonal relationships as democratic participation. There are at least four compelling reasons to expect to find such democratic participation in the public schools of America. First is the concept, written about by John Dewey (1916), that human beings will learn about democracy best when they experience it intellectually and emotionally during their formative years. Second is the fact that many popular educational innovations today require democratic social skills. We have in mind cooperative learning, students as conflict managers, peer tutoring and peer coaching, strategic planning, site-based management, restructuring for excellence, and interdisciplinary curricula in middle schools. Third is the theory that contemporary occupations require people who can work together collaboratively and that the main reason people fail in their jobs is that they lack human relations skills, principally the skill of empathy. Fourth is the value that democracy is as an end in itself, the moral way to behave in society.

The small district, with its tenacious reach into the community and its relative simplicity, seems to be ideal for fostering democratic participation. Why didn't we find more of it there, and what can be done to foster it? Those are the complex questions we will try to answer. We will take each kind of key participant, one by one, tell what we found out about them, and propose actions they might take to make small districts more democratic and educationally effective. Indeed, to meet the challenges of the small districts will require changes in how all of the key actors work together, including students, teachers, principals, superintendents, and board members.

## REFERENCES

Bane, M. J., & Ellwood, D. (1989, September). One-fifth of the nation's children: Why are they poor? *Science,* pp. 1047-1053.

Barker, R., & Gump, R. (1964). *Big school, small school: High school size and student behavior.* Stanford, CA: Stanford University Press.

Buber, M. (1958). *I and thou.* New York: Scribner.

Cremin, L. A. (1951). *The American common school: An historic conception.* New York: Columbia University, Teachers College, Bureau of Publications.

Dewey, J. (1916). *Democracy and education.* New York: Macmillan.

DeYoung, A. J. (1987). The status of American rural education research: An integrated review and commentary. *Review of Educational Research, 57*(2), 123-148.

DeYoung, A. J. (Ed.). (1991). *Rural education: Issues and practices.* New York: Garland.

Flanders, N. (1970). *Analyzing teaching behavior.* Reading, MA: Addison-Wesley.

Fuller, W. (1982). *The old country school: The story of rural education in the Middle West.* Chicago: University of Chicago Press.

Goodlad, J. (1984). *A place called school: Prospects for the future.* New York: Macmillan.

Hodgkinson, H. (1986, May 14). Here they come, ready or not: A special report. *Education Week,* pp. 14-37.

Least Heat Moon, W. (1982). *The blue highways: A journey into America.* New York: Fawcett Crest.

Nachtigal, P. (Ed.). (1982). *Rural education: In search of a better way.* Boulder, CO: Westview.

Peshkin, A. (1978). *Growing up American: Schooling and the survival of community.* Chicago: University of Chicago.

Peshkin, A. (1982). *The imperfect union: School consolidation and community conflict.* Chicago: University of Chicago Press.

Sher, J. (Ed.). (1977). *Education in rural America: A reassessment of conventional wisdom.* Boulder, CO: Westview.

Sher, J. (1981). *Rural education in urbanized nations: Issues and innovations.* Boulder, CO: Westview.

Smith, M., & Glass, G. (1979). *Relationship of class size to classroom processes, teacher satisfaction, and pupil affect.* San Francisco: Far West Educational Laboratory.

# 2

## Students

### PURSUING ACADEMIC EXCELLENCE

> Florenci is a city
> Stayton is a town
> Rockton is nothing
> But a hole in the ground
> —*A town saying about*
> *Rockton, down the hill from*
> *an open-pit copper mine*
> *(the actual town names*
> *have been changed)*

We were impressed by how important schools were to the majority of citizens of the small districts we visited. The river's vortex was indeed an apt metaphor. People of all ages, from 2 to 92, were at school often for social life, to vote and hold community meetings, and, infrequently, for something academic, but they went to the school most often for entertainment.

## STUDENTS AS ENTERTAINERS

In small districts, schools are entertainment centers, and students are the entertainers. This was true in every region of the country we visited. For example:

• On a rainy, gray January evening, off the Northern California coast, we sat with 450 cheering people of all ages to watch a basketball doubleheader. Few people in the audience left before the boys' varsity game was over.

• In bright and sunny Arizona three weeks later, we were told by the superintendent that 6,000 spectators in a town of 5,200 had attended a Christmas pageant performed by students of all ages.

• In a small Texas town on a cold, dreary Wednesday afternoon in February, an elementary school presented its student-performed musical variety show twice to accommodate all those who wanted to see it. The principal told us, "It's one of the high points of entertainment for the whole community, not just the parents."

• Close to the Mississippi River in a tiny Arkansas district, lucky enough to receive federal impact funds, we were interviewed about our trip around the United States on local television. The TV studio was in the brand-new high school; the channel was run by students. Our 17-year-old MC told us that between 400 and 500 people would watch this news and talk show.

• In Northern Wisconsin, a small district in the lake region has its own enclosed stadium for ice hockey, paid for with donations from the community. Starting in the fourth grade, boys compete against one another at grade level until they reach high school age and can play on the varsity team. Citizens of all ages and from all around flocked to the varsity games.

• In a small North Dakota district on an evening in early May when spring was barely showing its blossomy face, we walked without shoes on the shiny boards of a squeaky-new gymnasium floor with five school board members and the superintendent. "Our people have wanted an attractive place to go for entertainment during those long, cold winters," the head of the board told us. Eight hours earlier, in our two-on-one interview of the superintendent, he had complained about the poor financial condition of the district.

• And we suppose that, had we traveled in the fall, no doubt we would have seen the grandest American entertainment spectacle of all: high school football. We were told everywhere we went that upward of 75% of townspeople regularly attended the Friday night games.

*     *     *

The high schools, of course, were the most active entertainment centers of the small districts, and high school students were the primary entertainers. Some weeks, especially during the winter months, entertainment took place every night of the week except Sunday at the high school. In one small district on the shores of Lake Superior in Upper Michigan, we saw a musical variety show on Sunday afternoon. Sports events, musical concerts, art shows, and theatrical presentations were among the most popular entertainment. Parents, preschoolers, elementary students, grandparents, the extended family, and citizens at large, especially seniors, were the audiences. The majority of high school students acted as the entertainers; they were the athletes, cheerleaders, vendors, musicians, scorekeepers, mascots, artists, actors, stagehands, ushers, and cleanup crews. Nearly half of the teachers and most of their administrators acted as coaches, sponsors, advisers, directors, and supervisors, but it was the students who were at center stage.

## The Study

We interviewed a diverse sample of 212 working- and middle-class teenagers, including 104 girls and 108 boys. We talked with them singly, in pairs, in small groups, and in classes. We interviewed approximately 10 students individually in each district we visited. The students ranged in age from 13 to 18. We interviewed college-preparatory and vocationally oriented students, class officers, athletes, and informal leaders. We even spoke with a few high school students soon after they had received a paddling from the principal. We also made informal observations of student behavior in the community and formal observations of 50 minutes each in 30 secondary classrooms.

## Attitudes Toward the Small District

The theme of the vulnerable vortex came across in our interviews with the oldest students. The high school seniors felt ambivalent about their futures and sad about their towns. Although they enjoyed the social support of being at center stage of small-district life, they realized that they would have to move away from family and friends and the security of a close-knit community to pursue their adult careers.

As graduation neared, many seniors began to realize, perhaps for the first time, that they had been big fish in a small pond. In less than a year, they would move out of the spotlight on center stage to become one of many fish swimming in a large sea. Most of them also were conscious of their town's economic vulnerability and knew that they would never be able to obtain employment there.

Once their days as entertainers were over, they would not be able to find adult work. In one mining town with severe economic problems, a parent told us, "Kids must leave this town. If they don't, the girls will get pregnant and the boys will smoke dope and pump gas. There is nothing else for them here." One student told us, "I'd hate to see this town die, but it looks like it will." Another lamented, "This was a nice place to grow up; it makes me sad to see everything dying." One student with a glimmer of optimism said, "I won't live here during my adult years because there are too few opportunities, but maybe I'll retire here." We thought: Perhaps you'll be part of an audience for another generation of teenage entertainers.

We commenced the student interviews by asking for the best and worst things about school. The rank order of the most frequently occurring answers for the *best things* follows:

1. Lots of friends
2. Everybody knows everybody else
3. Small classes with individual attention
4. Sports, clubs, and other extracurricular activities
5. No drugs, muggings, or weapons
6. Caring attitudes of teachers and administrators

The rank order of the most frequently occurring answers for the *worst things* follows:

1. Too few electives or advanced courses
2. Teachers who don't care and aren't friendly
3. Alcohol abuse
4. Gossip and rumors about sexual misbehavior or drinking
5. Closed campus, particularly at lunch
6. Restrictive dress code

We went on to ask students how they felt about their small district—the school and its setting. Although they frequently started out by stating favorable sentiments, such as "there are good feelings here" and "I've got lots of friends," well over 50% soon pointed out how boring and uninteresting the academic part of school was. When we probed them specifically about their boredom and alienation, they spoke emotionally about particular classes and teachers, totalling, we surmise, about 30% of each student's classroom experiences. Most students lamented despairingly about at least two of their teachers.

The students seldom responded unhappily, however, toward the school as a whole, nor were they frustrated with extracurricular activities. In contrast, the majority of students we interviewed said that they "lived" to see their friends and to participate in extracurricular activities. The only students who showed some frustration with extracurricular events were those few intellectually oriented students in music or theater who complained about the extravagant value placed on boys' varsity sports in the community.

The small-district adolescents differed from their urban counterparts in their comfortable feelings of safety and security. About half of the schools we visited did not have locks on the lockers. Moreover, a considerable number of students told us about the muggings, knife fights, and handguns prominently present in inner-city schools. Apparently, they were trying to tell us how secure they felt in contrast to their urban counterparts. Unlike their urban counterparts, most small-district teenagers felt involved in extracurricular activities such as music, sports, theater, TV, and services or special interest clubs. Most of them were shining in their roles as entertainers. Only about 10% of students were clearly alienated from school, and many of those spoke of serious family disturbances. No student seemed to feel objectified or like an "It" in his or her role of community entertainer. Also, in contrast to urban students, small-district students encountered very few, if any, problems with hard drugs. Instead, we saw high school students almost everywhere actively campaigning against hard drugs. Alcohol, however, was not categorized as a hard drug and was being used widely.

## Corporal Punishment

Although we had not planned to ask about it, we unwittingly stumbled upon the use of the wooden paddle in a small-district high school in Tennessee. After school was over one Tuesday afternoon, we saw 19 high school students (18 boys and 1 girl) lined up outside the principal's office. We asked one of them, "What's the line for?" He just grinned without an answer. Another student in front of him turned and said, "We're waiting to get our swats from the principal," and they joked about full wallets or paperback books providing padding in their back pockets. We had just finished our interview with the principal and he hadn't mentioned anything about paddling to us. Not apparently frightened or even ill at ease, the students accepted two swats each behind the closed door of the principal's office.

A student explained to us, "We have a choice of either two swats or spending one hour after school in a detention study hall." Another said smiling, "We'd rather get hit twice than study!" Another said, "It doesn't hurt that much; for some of us it's a badge of honor." We walked away with a feeling of chagrin about this badge of honor and what these students were learning about the value of academic study. Perversely, even these marginal students were acting as entertainers, at least to one another.

After that, we spoke with most school administrators about their uses of corporal punishment and were surprised to find out how widely accepted paddling was, especially in elementary schools. One elementary principal in rural Illinois told us that only she, herself, administered the paddling, and that she typically spanked only "upper-grade boys to get their attention and to change their behavior." She did not paddle girls, and for the most part we found that to be true in most small districts. Another principal told us that in Texas the paddle itself must be made of wood, must be 17 inches long, four inches wide, and a half inch thick, and must not have holes in it. The devotees of the art of paddling call such holes "suck holes." Further-more, the district policy in Tennessee specifies that, before paddling one of the disobedient boys, the principal must ask the youngster about any bruises or bumps that he might already have on his underside and if there is any medical reason why he should not be paddled. After taking those precautions, the principal would tell the culprit to bend over and would hit him firmly twice on the buttocks. District policy usually stipulated that, in cases where the paddling did not change the wayward boy's behavior, the principal was to suspend him from school for a few days.

## Attitudes Toward Teachers

We also asked students about good and bad teaching in our inter-views. We asked them for behavioral examples, not for names of teachers. The rank order of the most frequently occurring answers for *good teaching* follows:

1. Gives students respect, is patient, and easy to get along with
2. Makes the subject interesting and fun, by involving students in activities and demonstrations
3. Tells jokes and smiles a lot; good sense of humor
4. Listens to student questions and makes changes in class to help students learn

The rank order of the most frequently occurring answers for *bad teaching* follows:

1. Low respect for students, lacks patience, and treats you as if you are stupid
2. Seldom smiles, very serious and stern, and uses either too harsh or too permissive discipline
3. Doesn't care about or pay attention to individuals; not helpful
4. Doesn't explain well, lazy, hands out work sheets and tests; you have to learn everything on your own
5. Has favorites; favors the smart students or one sex over another

From our interviews with students, we surmise that about 30% of teachers in the small districts we visited were not valued by the students. We also surmise that bad teaching from the students' points of view more frequently came from teachers who did *not* take part in extracurricular activities than from those who acted as advisers and supervisors of out-of-class activities. About 30% of teachers made school boring for most students, and at times their behavior added stress to the students' lives. The students viewed those teachers as lacking *respect* for adolescents, unwilling to go half way to establish *rapport* with them, lacking a *sense of humor,* not *caring* much about teaching and learning, and *playing favorites.*

Those findings are similar to an inquiry made by the senior author of 245 urban and suburban teenagers 25 years previously (see Schmuck, 1965, for details). The earlier interviews revealed that the adolescents were concerned with "making sense out of the multiple social demands of parents, teachers, and peers, while striving to become an autonomous and integrated individual." With regard to their teachers, metropolitan youth of the 1960s were most concerned with the following: (a) *Teachers not getting to know the students,* for example: "We get too little personal attention from our teachers." "Teachers don't care if they get to know you or not." "Our teachers are like machines; they just 'spiel' out information." (b) *Teachers lacking interest in teaching and youth,* for example: "He comes to class unprepared." "Most of my teachers care if we learn, but two sure don't." "They aren't even interested in what they are teaching." (c) *Teachers showing partiality for particular students,* for example: "They have their pets." "Many girls get away with murder in this school, simply because they are girls." "You have to 'brown up' the teachers to do well."

We were struck with how similar the urban adolescents of the 1960s sounded compared with their counterparts in small districts in the 1990s. Indeed, our study proved to us that American adolescents in small districts today do not have attitudes toward teachers substantially different than their urban counterparts of more than a generation ago. Instead of being concerned about the curriculum, homework, and tests, most students think much more, we believe, about their interpersonal relationships with teachers. They want their teachers to respect them, to engage them in joyful activities in the classroom, to have fun with them, and to respond flexibly in helping them learn. The most salient inner concerns of adolescents have been and continue to be interpersonal and social-emotional.

As we traveled the American countryside to visit small districts, we read some of the most popular reform reports of the 1980s. We read, for example, *A Nation at Risk* by the National Commission on Excellence in Education (1983), *Action for Excellence* by the Task Force on Education for Economic Growth (1983), and *A Nation Prepared: Teachers for the 21st Century* by the Task Force on Teaching as a Profession (1986). We became depressed as we discovered how far away from the students' reality those reports were.

It became quite clear to us that adolescents' views have not been taken into consideration by the literature of school reform in the 1980s. The reform reports focused on the intellectual competence and the academic performance of teachers, *not* their compassion, empathy, self-esteem, respect, or love of young people. The national reports emphasized teachers' intelligence, academic achievement, grade point average, course work within the liberal arts, and years of college education. They did not focus on the social-emotional characteristics of teachers to which the adolescents themselves were so constantly alert. Why haven't the high-level national committee members talked with the students? Those young people whom we interviewed—all around the country—were not thinking about their teachers' subject matter competence, breadth of knowledge, or ability to do well in college classrooms. We never heard students rejoice over their teacher's grade point average in college. Rather, they praised teachers who were human beings, who showed trust, respect, and understanding to them.

## Importance of the Peer Group

What's the "one best thing" about school? Being with friends wins hands down. That was true in the 1960s when the senior author interviewed metropolitan teenagers; it was true when Benham, Giesen, and Oakes (1980) gave questionnaires to 11,767 secondary students in seven states; and it was true when we traveled the blue highways of America a few years ago.

The most repeated peer interaction we saw among adolescents was cruising: students, clad in jeans, T-shirts, and sweatshirts, driving cars and trucks through the center of town on Friday, Saturday, and even Sunday nights between 9:00 p.m. and midnight. After athletic events at school or after a movie, they were out there to entertain one another. The ritual, just as well known to suburban and urban adolescents, was variously called "cruising the gut," "shooting the loop," "roving the strip," and even "cruising the mall." In a Tennessee town, we saw adolescents driving through a large shopping mall, instead of the old downtown, apparently because, from their point of view, that was "where the action was" now. Even in the small towns of rural America, where distances are not as great as in the cities, cars are king. Adolescents do not walk to school, to the movies, to softball, to the hamburger joint, or to a date. They seldom even think of the pleasure of a stroll in the countryside just to experience nature.

*Classroom Observations*

Of the 30 secondary classes we observed, 22 were clearly controlled almost constantly by the teacher. We saw teachers standing up front lecturing to rows of students with only occasional student talk as a response to the teachers' questions. That was as true in a class of 12 as it was in a class of 26. Most teachers we observed apparently had not themselves been influenced by one of Mark Twain's favorite sayings, which we saw printed neatly in calligraphy on the wall of a junior high class in Missouri, "If we were supposed to talk more than listen, we'd have two mouths and one ear." From the students' point of view, the teachers wanted students to listen to them, but the teachers did not often apply Twain's maxim to themselves when they were teaching.

Again and again we saw teachers, handpicked by their principals as good teachers, who were frustrated by their inability to motivate students to work hard on the curriculum. One ninth-grade teacher in Western Illinois reached the end of his rope one Thursday while we sat silently in the back of the room. He scolded the 26 students during a health class for not completing an assignment on time. Actually, 13 students had completed the assignment and 13 had not. "I'm disappointed," he said. "I thought more of you would have your reports done. You are being prepared for life. Will you tell your boss? 'I'm sorry; I didn't get it done!' You must be responsible to get your homework done on time. Mom can't do it; Dad can't do it. You must be responsible to do your own work on time."

In that angry vein, the teacher castigated the students for their lack of achievement, striving, and academic productivity. They were reticent. He did not pause in his tirade, nor did he ask them for their thoughts or feelings. After 25 minutes of venting anger, the teacher directed the students—all 26—to work alone and silently at their desks completing the homework assignment, apparently having forgotten that half of them had already completed the assignment. He was no closer to communicating with the students after the tirade than before it. Later that day, we saw one of the students in the class entertaining his friends by wearing a cap on which was printed the inscription, "Homework causes brain damage."

In 8 classes, among the 30, the teacher did plan some sort of student-to-student talk. Twice we saw students sitting in pairs and responding cooperatively to the teacher's questions or directions. Four times we saw students in small groups working together on a project. Twice we saw high school English teachers, one in Missouri and one in Minnesota, engaging both sides of their students' brains in learning.

The teacher in Missouri carried out a poignant, thoroughly absorbing discussion with 15 students about a short story by Ann Beattie titled, "Imagine a Day at the End of Your Life." The story concerns a man growing old, who has felt subsumed by his family. He finds himself at last by scrutinizing nature, smelling the wet grass, seeing the trees turn green, and listening to the birds and the breeze. The teacher sat relaxed with the students and informally prodded them to discuss their reactions to the story. He presented his own thoughts and feelings but encouraged them to talk about theirs, and they did. Together, the teacher and students discussed how they now lived and how they wanted to live; they probed the meaning of their lives together—a poignant portrait of human exchange.

In another class in the northwest corner of Minnesota, we saw students work in small groups of two to four students to create stories with illustrations that they were to read to kindergartners. The teacher had the students read children's books and discuss the sorts of things that interest 5-year-olds, such as animals that act like people, learning through active experience, and everything coming out OK in the end. The students had one week to create the stories outside class. They were to write the script, draw the pictures, and plan an oral presentation to 5-year-olds.

On the day we visited class, some of the small groups were presenting stories to their classmates. The teacher already had announced that only three stories were to be read to the 5-year-olds, and the class would have to vote on the top three stories in the class. After each story was presented, the students took notes and did some tentative rating. Later, the whole class would decide on the top three stories.

The stories we saw presented to peers were delightful and creative. The student presenters were poised, articulate, and well organized.

More important, their peers were captivated, enthusiastic, silly, and having fun. The teacher, mostly silent, sat in the back of the room observing. He spoke only to call up each group in turn and to remind the students of their responsibility to select the top three stories.

In an elementary school in Illinois, we saw a group of 11 second graders delving into the moral choices and innocence or guilt of Jack in "Jack and the Beanstalk." The students were actively engaged in discussion where, as the teacher said, "there are no right or wrong answers." When we interviewed the students about their future life choices, one young girl had taken the issue of moral choice very seriously. She told us, "When I grow up I'm going to be a lawyer, judge, or jury." This was an exciting class and students listened well to each other. It was, however, a special class for talented and gifted students. They were removed from their regular classrooms to participate in the Junior Great Books Program, which stresses using interpretive questions, articulating ideas, learning from each other, and putting ideas on paper. While the class was very exciting, we were discouraged that only a few students were able to participate in such an important discussion. This was an "exceptional" class. We wondered why it couldn't be an "ordinary" class.

## The Curriculum

Outdated texts and irrelevant curricula have become the norm in America's small-town schools. Most districts rely heavily upon the materials designed for urban and suburban populations that dominate commercial publishing and have little meaning for life in rural and small-town America. In one elementary classroom we visited, the students were reading a basal text that had a story about a boy living in an apartment building. The teacher reported that she was well into the comprehension section of the text before she realized most of her students didn't know what an apartment building was. They had never seen an apartment building and missed the main point of the story.

One obstacle to curricula that reflects the lives of rural and small-town children is the lack of funds, skill, and time for rural educators to create relevant curricula. The curriculum must give students a sense of options about their adult lives. Too often, because of the economic despair in many small towns, school is seen as the way either to prepare students to leave their community for employment somewhere else or to remain in their own town only to live on the fringes of society. The best curriculum, we think, equips students to live successful, complete lives in their own community or in an urban community. Small-town schools seem to do neither; they do not provide students with skills to manage their lives successfully in other communities, nor do they provide options for students to engage as productive persons in the development of their own communities.

## Student Councils

About 20% of the high school students we interviewed were student council officers. All of them had been elected by their peers to serve on the student council. We were curious to know how they thought the councils were contributing to their schools. We also wanted to know whether their participation on the councils might be enhancing their motivation to pursue academic excellence.

In general, we found high participation of students in the extracurricular life of the school, but we uncovered little influence from students on important academic matters. The elected student leaders told us that, although they were busily engaged in three or four extracurricular activities, they had little voice in influencing how teaching and learning operated at their school. The sort of activity they did influence included operating concessions at athletic events, organizing homecoming events, designing a schedule of schoolwide assemblies, procuring the music for dances, and persuading the principal to allow one day in the spring for students to wear Bermuda shorts.

A high school principal in Montana lamented that this year the student council had been particularly inactive. He told us, "I tried to get them motivated, but they just refused to do anything." We asked him for an example. "Well," he said, "student councils usually get a Christmas tree for the school. This year I mentioned it to council members in November, but they didn't bother getting one. So there was no Christmas tree."

In stark contrast to our repeated finding of low student influence over academic matters in secondary schools, we did find a high school in Mississippi that still was benefiting from earlier contributions by the student council. The district, racially segregated in 1970, had been successfully desegregated. The administrators arranged for leaders of the student councils of the black and the white schools to meet and to establish school policies and programs. As a consequence, the students had an influential voice in shaping the policies of their new school; they produced a Student Handbook, which was endorsed by the administrators. Today that school district still is an exemplary case of racial desegregation in the deep South.

On our visit of just a few years ago, however, we found *no* school, not even the exemplary one in Mississippi, in which the student council played any important part in academic life. They dealt only with entertainment and social events. Throughout America, the administrators of small districts admitted that the student council was ineffective if not inoperative. A few schools provided leadership training to students but, in most small districts, when a student council existed, it was mainly a perfunctory and pallid sham of representative democracy.

## PORTRAITS OF THREE STUDENTS

Northwest of the source of the Mississippi River and east of the Red River, where the stalwart farmers on one side have built dikes higher than the farmers on the other side, thereby keeping the floods on the other side of the river, we visited a small Minnesota town with about 1,000 residents. On the flat prairie land surrounding the town, farmers grow sugar beets, seed potatoes, and various grains. The town itself, made up of small, modest, one-story brick and frame houses, has the necessary services: a grocery store, a gas station with a mechanic, three small restaurants, a bakery, the telephone company, a newspaper office, and a small motel.

We met with Jim Ferris, Ted Grimes, and Ned Schulz, three senior high school boys, in fifth-hour study hall. All had lived in or near this town and had gone to school in this small district from kindergarten to the 12th grade. We talked with them because they were the only students in that study hall at that time. They told a story of their school experiences quite different than the stories told by the student council officers we had interviewed earlier in the day. These were not student leaders, nor were they the town's entertainers. They were barely holding on to their place in the district.

Talking with Jim, Ted, and Ned, we felt like a dentist pulling teeth; they grunted, responded with barely audible yes's and no's, and averted their eyes from us, though they sent glances among themselves and giggled frequently. Although they clearly were uncomfortable talking to us, we pursued our primitive conversation with them for the full 50 minutes of the study period. "At least I have an excuse now for not doing my history," was Ted's flippant response when we thanked them at the end of our interview. So much for our contribution to academic excellence in small districts, we thought.

What about their future? Ned was reluctantly going to "give the local community college a try"; Ted intended to sign up for the military, probably the army; and Jim was going to learn how to be an auto mechanic, but he wasn't really sure how he would do that. He said, "First, I'll get a job in a fast-food restaurant—that's about the only job here except for pumping gas—and then I guess I'll have enough money to go to mechanic's school." He had no clue, however, where a mechanic's school was or what its course of study would be. Less than one month from graduation, Jim didn't know that there was a vocational training program available in auto mechanics at a nearby community college.

We asked them about their experiences in school. "Teachers are not very good here," Ned said, as though he had school experiences elsewhere. "They don't listen and they don't explain well. I had a hard time in math, but my father helped me." Ted piped up, "The good teachers are those that listen and like to have fun, but there's not a lot of those." Ted went on, "I don't know why English is required for four years in high school. I'm not going to read dumb novels—it's just a waste of time. I'd rather be working or hunting."

Ned and Jim nodded their heads in agreement. Jim said, "The kids in this school are OK, but lots of them are snobs. I play on the baseball team and that's OK, but even then we have to play with another school. There's not even enough kids here to make up a baseball team." We asked, "What do you like best, Jim, about being on the baseball team?" He responded, "Getting out of school early when we travel." The other two laughed.

"Do you plan to leave this town or do you see yourself living here?" we asked. "We're going to get out of this town," all three quickly answered almost in unison. Yet, after a few moments of silence, Ted said thoughtfully, "but I don't mind living here. I could see myself coming back after the army. I just want to see what other places are like." Much later, we guessed that by then he might have seen Saudi Arabia. We wondered what he thought of that.

The ambivalence of high school girls and boys toward staying in their small-district towns was virtually universal among the students we interviewed. After all, their lives in small-town America might be boring for six hours a day in class, but it was familiar and secure. They had their social lives and local entertainment. They could also see the troubles of the urban world through television and movies. We think many of the students we interviewed felt down deep that they'd like very much to stay in their small-district towns.

Jim, Ted, and Ned were C students. They were unusual interviewees for us, because administrators and teachers usually would select the A and B students for us to interview. We just happened upon these three boys in their fifth-hour study hall and asked the teacher who supervised them if we could interview them. The teacher quickly agreed and left us alone with the boys. Our finding them was similar to how we just happened upon the 19 students in Tennessee who were waiting in line to be paddled. The principal of that school had not intended for us to interview those students.

Just the same, we were sobered by the fact that what these alienated youth said about school life was actually not very different than what their "better performing" peers were saying. Save for very few classes and teachers, academic life was boring and meaningless. Only about 10% of the students we interviewed commented on how interested or engaged they were in a subject they were studying. It was rare for a student to praise a story, an exercise, a discussion, or an experiment. It was even rarer for us to observe the sort of psychological energy and joy in learning that we saw in the two high school English classes described earlier. We concluded that, by and large, the students in small districts are no more likely than their urban and suburban counterparts to be pursing academic excellence.

## TARGETS OF CHANGE

In *The Predictable Failure of Educational Reform,* Seymour Sarason (1990) argues convincingly that real reform won't occur in education until we stop accepting the educational system as it has been and is. The key to effective change is radical change in the power relationships among the administrators, teachers, and students in the school and between teachers and students in the classroom. In particular, he focuses upon power relationships between students, on the one hand, and the adult educators, on the other. Students will begin to pursue academic excellence enthusiastically when they are empowered to influence decision making in the classroom and the school.

Our visit to 25 small districts across the United States convinced us that Sarason's insights about asymmetrical power relationships between adult educators and students is a major source of the students' lack of enthusiasm for academic learning. Cast in the role of community entertainers, moreover, students learn to value their performances in extracurricular activities over their classroom performances. Spending time in classes is a required sacrifice that must be made so that students can entertain the local citizenry. Students' power in small districts thus is the power of the court jester admired for entertainment but not taken seriously as a participant in the ruling class.

The most salient concerns of adolescents, all over America, have to do with their power relationships with peers, parents, teachers, administrators, and the community. Underlying those concerns is their search for identity and self-esteem. The constructive engagement of 13- to 18-year-olds in the following activities would begin to alter the status quo.

## Teacher Selection and Assessment

There is widespread interest today in the site-based management of schools. That interest is supported by the concept of teacher empowerment. The argument is that, if teachers become engaged in managing their own school, then they also will do a more enthusiastic job of teaching. Site-based management, however, can also apply to student empowerment. Students might go to class more enthusiastically if they were influential in selecting and assessing teachers.

We believe that adolescent students should be integrally engaged in selecting and assessing teachers. Although including them might be impossible when hiring late in the summer, students should serve on selection committees, both to interview and to observe prospective candidates for teaching positions in their school. There should be at least three or four students on the selection committee, because one or two can be too easily co-opted or stifled by the adults. The students could form their own selection committee separate from the teachers, with both the student committee and the teacher committee reporting to a schoolwide selection committee. The students should be allowed to interview candidates by themselves without administrators and teachers present, and they should be allowed to remain anonymous in making their ratings of the candidates. Most important, prospective teachers should have to teach a lesson or two in front of a class of students whose opinions will be heard during the selection procedure.

In both the interviews and the teaching demonstrations, the students should fill out rating forms. The forms should incorporate what we know about student attitudes toward teachers. The students should, for example, rate candidates on how much respect for students they show, how interesting they are, whether they smile and joke, whether they listen to students, and whether they appear to be helpful. Those criteria should be made known to the candidates ahead of time so that they will be aware of the emphasis on students' opinions in the school. Candidates should be prodded to articulate their philosophy and strategies of teaching to the students so that the students can judge how effectively the candidates will work with them in the classroom and in the school.

Students also should help assess the probationary teachers. Every six weeks, a formal "Class Reaction Inventory" should be given to all students in the classes of the probationary teachers. A committee of students should collect and analyze the data. The probationary teacher would be expected to leave the room during the data collection, allowing 30 minutes or so for a student to administer the questionnaire. Data later would be fed back to that teacher by members of the student committee. The probationary teachers would be expected to discuss how they might attempt to improve their teaching performance during the next six weeks.

Students also should be regularly asked by a teachers' committee or the principal—perhaps near the end of each semester—for information about good and bad teaching. There are several ways the information could be transmitted. The committee or principal could administer a "Class Reaction Inventory" similar to the one used on probationary teachers. They could then interview a random selection of students about a class to get more information. The teachers' committee or principal also could, perhaps once a month, interview small groups of students about their teachers' strong and weak points. In the discussions, the committee or principal should ask students to give specific examples of teaching behaviors that are helpful and unhelpful for student learning. The committee or principal should later give summaries of the students' comments to their teachers as an impetus to upgrade instruction and to democratize school life.

## Student Councils

We also believe that administrators and teachers should turn their attention to empowering student councils. Well-functioning councils give students an opportunity to experience democracy firsthand: Students can learn to lead effectively, to work in groups cooperatively, and to act responsibly on behalf of the school. Moreover, making it legitimate for councils to give formal advice to administrators and teachers about the curriculum and instruction can help in school reform efforts.

In one district we visited in Wisconsin, the superintendent, several teachers, and some parents accompanied the student representatives from the high school to a statewide leadership conference. There, the adults and the students exchanged their attitudes about some of the limitations in the curriculum. Those students felt good about the important contributions they were making to their schools' programs. Unfortunately, too few of the secondary administrators and teachers with whom we talked truly believed that students ought to be engaged in criticizing their school's curriculum.

For students to be empowered, they will have to be viewed by administrators and teachers as bona fide organizational participants, not as the mere objects of education. As Sarason (1990) has so nicely argued, adult efforts at school reform can falter when students intentionally or unconsciously sabotage attempts by the professionals to work in new ways. We have studied elementary staffs, for example, that were attempting to move from a self-contained structure to team teaching. In some of those schools, the students' expectations to have their own homeroom teacher were so strong that they resisted going along with the teachers' efforts at individualizing instruction and platooning the students into various groups. In another instance, we observed secondary schools in Oregon in which the staff's plans for student government went awry because of student apathy.

The major problem is that teachers and administrators can become so preoccupied with their own work and responsibilities that they lose sensitivity to students' preferences, concerns, and attitudes. In many of the small districts we visited, the teachers, administrators, and students alike had sought isolation from the two other groups to avoid debilitating and unproductive disagreement over different values. In previous visits, however, to districts in California, Oregon, and Washington, we found a few promising examples of student councils:

• In a newly formed middle school (grades six to eight), two students from each homeroom were selected by their peers to serve on the council. Four teachers joined the whole council at a weekend retreat at one of the teacher's vacation cottages to establish procedures for the work of the council. A counselor from the school also trained the students in skills of communication and running meetings effectively. The council members planned several schoolwide projects. One was to mount a special fair in the gymnasium to welcome incoming sixth graders each year and to acquaint them with the academic offerings of the school. Another was to interview both their fellow students and a sample of teachers about the strengths and weaknesses of the academic program. On one occasion, leaders from the council were invited to a graduate class for educational administrators at a university. Their visit to the university strengthened the cohesiveness of the student leaders and their commitment toward engaging in academic excellence.

• At a junior high school (grades seven to nine), the principal asked all of the teachers to act as counselors to students at least part time. She did this in the context of introducing a "house system" into the school. Each house consisted of 18 students and one counselor-teacher. The teachers worked one-to-one with the students and used an instructional module with the entire group of 18 titled: *School Life and Organizational Psychology* by Arends et al. (1981). That module consists of a text for students and a handbook for teachers with duplicating masters. The module units include topics such as the self and the organization, living our lives in organizations, human motives and organization, groups in organizations, roles in groups, and norms in groups. Students kept a diary throughout the course in which they explained how the ideas they were studying applied to themselves and to their school as an organization.

Late in the year, the principal asked every house to select four representatives (two girls and two boys) to take part in a weekend retreat at her farm. There they discussed how the academic climate of their junior high could be strengthened. Some ideas from those discussions, such as student tutors, new courses, and student-managed learning centers, became a part of the school the next year.

Some senior high schools also have tried out various types of governing structures through which students have been empowered to make decisions about academic matters. The most successful one we observed consisted of a bicameral structure in which the teachers' senate was independent of the student council. The student council itself was organized through a homeroom structure and integrated by what Rensis Likert (1961) called a "link-pin" structure; that is, each homeroom had two representatives in the council. At the apex of the link-pin structure for the whole school was the principal's cabinet, which was made up of four officers from the teachers' senate and four student officers. The cabinet sought to settle differences that could arise between the two halves of the bicameral structure.

## Community Development

We believe, finally, that administrators and teachers should find ways for students to serve their communities as an integral part of their school experience. The work of secondary students in their communities might be especially easy for small communities to accept, because the high school already serves as the people's gathering place and as the community social center. Although we already have had the community school movement in America since the 1950s, that movement has not typically empowered students to take a central role in community development.

In one community, residents had become concerned about the high school students' apathy, lack of responsibility, and even vandalism in the downtown. Members of the business community asked the high school principal to "control those high school kids better." The principal wisely suggested that they were "our" kids and created a community forum to discuss the problems and to come up with possible solutions. Thus the schools, the business community, parents, and other citizens tackled the problem of student responsibility together. The following year, there was almost no vandalism reported in the downtown. It is possible to link community and school in productive ways so that adolescents are viewed and treated as responsible community members.

There are a number of avenues, small and large, by which secondary students could contribute to community development. For example, students could work in day-care centers and preschools. They could clean up the streets and alleys or otherwise beautify the face of the town. They could act as big brother or sister to younger children and serve as cross-age tutors to middle school students. They could write columns for the local newspaper, put on a radio broadcast on PBS, and read to senior citizens in nursing homes or write letters for them. What is possible is limited only by our imagination. Students themselves, through their classes in social studies or as a part of student council, could generate their own plans for community development.

It is particularly critical that America's decaying small towns today find alternative sources of financial support. We believe that it is worth a try to bring students into problem-solving discussions about local economic development. Perhaps the students, free to some extent of the psychological constraints of community tradition, will come up with a few feasible ways to establish new industries in small-town America. We could make John Dewey smile again if somehow his problem-solving project method could be applied to economic development at the grass roots.

## REFERENCES

Arends, R., et al. (1981). *School life and organizational psychology.* New York: Teachers College Press.

Benham, B., Giesen, P., & Oakes, J. (1980). A study of schooling: Students' experiences in schools. *Phi Delta Kappan, 61*(5), 337-340.

Likert, R. (1961). *New patterns of management.* New York: McGraw-Hill.

National Commission on Excellence in Education. (1983). *A nation at risk.* Washington, DC: Government Printing Office.

Sarason, S. B. (1990). *The predictable failure of educational reform.* San Francisco: Jossey-Bass.

Schmuck, R. (1965). Concerns of contemporary adolescents. *Bulletin of the National Association of Secondary School Principals, 49*(300), 19-28.

Task Force on Education for Economic Growth. (1983). *Action for excellence.* Denver, CO: Education Commission of the States.

Task Force on Teaching as a Profession. (1986). *A nation prepared: Teachers for the 21st century.* New York: Carnegie Corporation of New York.

# 3

## Teachers

### GETTING BEYOND
### BITTERSWEET BELONGING

This school requires no physical fitness program.
Everyone here gets enough exercise:
> Jumping to conclusions,
> Carrying things too far,
> Dodging responsibility,
> Flying off the handle,
> And pushing their luck.
>> —*Poster in teachers' lounge*

Our odyssey started on the day after New Year's, 1989, when we left our home in Eugene, Oregon, in a 22-foot Tioga RV we had nicknamed "the White Tortoise" for its want of speed.

We crawled south toward the sun and warm weather, climbing over the ominous Siskiyou mountains, the snowy barrier separating

Oregon from California. Leaving snow behind, we drove further south through the fertile valleys of California, reading *The Grapes of Wrath* aloud, then east across what Steinbeck called the "sun-rotted mountains and deserts" of the Southwest and through Texas and Louisiana into Mississippi.

Then we zigzagged north along the Mississippi River, the liquid roadway from Louisiana to Minnesota, through the cotton-rich delta into the drought-stricken corn and wheat fields of the Midwest to cold Lake Superior. We turned west across Minnesota, North Dakota, Montana, Idaho, and Washington and finally crossed the great Columbia River early in June, as we read the last pages of Steinbeck's masterpiece and rested our eyes on snow-capped Mount Hood.

Because *The Grapes of Wrath* first was published in 1939, bookstores all over were touting a beautiful 50th-year special anniversary edition. On public radio, Studs Terkel, who had prepared the foreword for the new edition, told how contemporary the book is today. We, too, were impressed with the contemporary truth of the novel. Even though many Americans seem to be rejoicing in an apparent economic prosperity, most small districts we visited actually were suffering economic depressions nearly as severe as that which the Joads encountered in their dusty Oklahoma village during the Great Depression.

Furthermore, the Joads' dedication to family and community, their frustration with trying to cope with dire economic circumstances, and their unending hope for a better, more humane society reminded us of the many teachers we had been meeting who were equally *dedicated, frustrated,* and *hopeful.*

The shared reading of Steinbeck helped us in another way. For the first time, we both recognized how skillfully he had alternated chapters between the story of the Joads and the economic plight of the United States during the 1930s. Like Peter Breughel the Elder, Steinbeck had portrayed individuals of the Joad family in the foreground against the demographic changes and mass migration patterns of the background. We wanted to emulate him by presenting portraits of individuals, like the teachers we present here, against the backdrop of the economic, organizational, and social conditions of small districts. We also adopted some of Steinbeck's passionate optimism for the human condition, by choosing to describe the exemplary educators we met and by offering a few action ideas to deal with the big problems of small districts.

## PORTRAITS OF FIVE TEACHERS

We were favorably impressed with many of the 119 teachers we interviewed and observed, but 5 were particularly outstanding. Judy Landry, a graduate of the counterculture in San Francisco, had retreated to a less crowded life to teach elementary school in a small district, still hopeful of a more cooperative world. After watching Judy work, we expected only the very best of small-district teachers. Betty Robinson, dedicated and charming, taught an attentive and appreciative elementary class of very poor children in the deep South. We were uplifted by her dedication and hope. Gary and Karen Ritter, conscientious, sensitive, and profoundly frustrated humanists, worked in the drought-stricken middle of the Midwest. We were depressed by the frustration and self-doubt of these outstanding teachers. Finally, Peter Olsen, with leather jacket and motorcycle, taught high school students to perform Ibsen's *Hedda Gabler* for an audience of conservative Scandinavian farmers in the Upper Midwest. We were enchanted by the playful delight of this mature young adult and his dedication to his students.

### Judy Landry

Our first stop after leaving Oregon was on the coast of Northern California. We were pleased in general with the psychological climate we found. The superintendent, warm and articulate, seemed to be practicing participatory management, working closely and collaboratively with his administrators in a district leadership team. The board members were conscientious, knowledgeable, and supportive of the educators' endeavors. The principals apparently were striving to give teachers voice in managing the school. An effective alternative-school program was nurturing 25 students, who otherwise would *not* have made it in high school, to learn to succeed and eventually to graduate. Nothing in this district, however, was quite as impressive as the teaching of Judy Landry.

A white, blond, mature, and athletic woman, typically dressed in slacks, 39 years old, Judy was active, vivacious, and smiling. With a fourth- and fifth-grade combination of primarily white but a few black and Hispanic students, she bounced around the room from small group to small group, giving encouragement, information, and frequent reinforcement. On the colorful walls of the room, student-made signs read: "Be Kind, Be Cooperative, Be an Active Listener, Take Turns, Respect One Another." She told us, "I use a lot of group work, and I'm careful not to stream according to achievement. So I usually have fourth and fifth graders work together in the same groups, and I change the composition of the groups from time to time."

Judy Landry had been teaching in that same district for 12 years, and she didn't want to leave. Having attended college at the pinnacle of student activism in the early 1970s, she had been an integral part of the counterculture movement in San Francisco's Haight-Ashbury neighborhood. After teaching for a few years in the inner city of Oakland, and after a brief stint in a master's degree program, she decided to retreat to a simpler, less hurried life far from the city.

She told us, "I moved north with other refugees of San Francisco. Some of them stopped just above Sausalito and went no further. Others stopped and put down roots in the Sonoma Valley." With a poetic flair, she exclaimed, "Up Highway 128 we went past Boonville, then Mendocino, and north even to Oregon. We revered the whale, the redwood, the alfalfa sprout, the thrown pot, meditation, and sensitivity training. Now, we're growing older and more seasoned."

We were impressed with how vigorously Judy and some of her mobile urban colleagues still were seeking cooperation, freedom, and community, even in this small town of conservative farmers, fishers, and loggers.

Judy Landry had carried her past into the present; her class was a virtual buzz of activity, with small groups chatting enthusiastically and cooperatively. Here or there individual youngsters worked alone reading, drawing, and filling in work sheets. We could not easily distinguish the fourth graders from the fifth graders. A few students in front of a computer screen were concentrating on a problem-solving activity. Everywhere we looked, boys and girls were seriously working together. Now and then, Judy would redirect a student whose attention had wandered, or she would tell the whole class to reduce the noise level.

At lunch, she explained how wonderful the staff were at her school and how lucky she was to be there. We observed a handful of her colleagues and found them too to be using small group discussions in their classes. We were inspired by the happy emotional vibrations in the school, by the smiles, laughter, enthusiasm, and cooperation. Judy said, "This is a very cooperative staff; it is a staff, too, that knows how to use staff development. We really help each other and work together well." Later she told us, "Society is down on teachers too much; the attacks in some of the reform reports are unreasonable." We agreed.

We were enlivened by Judy and her colleagues, so much so that we looked forward to the remainder of our trip to 24 other small districts with anticipation and excitement. We thought: Perhaps the teachers of small districts really are teaching students how to live well in a democracy. Perhaps smaller districts really are better than the bigger ones. Perhaps teachers are more highly respected in small districts than in metropolitan districts. Perhaps small is beautiful!

Wrong! To make a long story short, Judy Landry and her colleagues were virtually one of a kind, a special breed. Out of the 119 teachers we interviewed and observed, only 10 showed that they even recognized the term *cooperative learning,* and 5 were in Judy's school. Only 20 teachers among the 119 acknowledged having students work in small groups that were not ability groups. Indeed, teachers actually apologized for their use of group work, saying that it was their "last resort" for dealing with difficult students. Fortunately, we did not know all of that as we optimistically drove south, away from Judy Landry's school district.


*Betty Robinson*


After driving south almost to the Mexican border, we turned east across the brown Southwest, visiting small districts in Arizona, New

Mexico, and Texas. Then, toward the end of February, we drove into Louisiana to visit a small district in the economically devastated Mississippi Delta.

From the rear of a large fourth-grade classroom in a very old, dilapidated building, we watched 25 children, 23 black and 2 white, work in a large U-shaped seating arrangement facing the teacher. A few children glanced at us inquisitively but no one spoke to us.

Betty Robinson, a 38-year-old black woman, slender and vivacious, with her hair pulled back in a bun, was passing around copies of the *Weekly Reader* saying, "We shall read about animal experimentation today. Remember when we talked about this before?" A few students nodded as her eyes caught theirs. She raised questions, reviewing the entire article before they read it. She had provided what devotees of Madeline Hunter call an "anticipatory set"; she had prepared them for active reading.

The students read the article silently. There was hardly a sound, not a whisper, only the pitter-patter of a steady rain on the windows. We could hear the sounds of cars passing on the dirt road outside, but inside the room you could have heard a pin drop.

After five minutes of silence, Betty said, "Look at me, please, when you are finished reading." Already we could see a few eyeballs peering in Betty's direction. She said, "I'm beginning to see some eyes; that's good!" She waited patiently for another minute and then began a series of rapid-fire questions. As the students responded, she lavished immediate praise while uttering each responding child's first name.

Betty moved quickly around the U-shaped seating formation. She stood always, however, at the center of attraction, smiling and encouraging. There was no hand raised in peer competition. The students seemed to understand that they were expected to respond when her eyes met theirs. She would stop to face a student and ask another question about animal experimentation. When the student hesitated, she waited patiently and sometimes offered a helping hint. When the student answered correctly, she praised the student. When the student answered incorrectly, she smiled, said nothing, and went on to another student. Her pace was quick and steady, but also patient; the students were attentive and apparently secure.

Like 70% of teachers we interviewed in small districts, Betty Robinson had been born and raised in the neighborhood. The eldest of 13 children whose parents were sharecroppers, she and three of her siblings had attended college. Betty's two college-educated brothers had moved to New Orleans, her college-educated sister to Baton Rouge, but she had returned to her hometown soon after college. "I came to teach here in this school, where I went to school, because my community needed me. I had three job offers from larger districts in the cities for more money, but I was born and raised here and I have strong ties of loyalty."

As she spoke of her dedication and commitment to her hometown, images of the area's serious poverty vividly ran through our minds: boarded-up stores, weeds and vines covering rusted-out fenders and motors of junked cars, matchbox houses in dreary, rainy February without windows or paint, streets without signs, children with holes in their shoes playing outside. The nameplate on Betty's school, which read "Boo - - - T. W - sh - - - gton," offered a tangible and vivid metaphor of the district's missing parts: money, jobs, and white middle-class students. The state's unemployment rate was the highest in the nation; the county's unemployment rate, the highest in the state. Mechanization had come to the farms, so there was little work left for the sharecroppers.

Betty's town stood next to an ox-bow lake, formed more than a century before as the ever-winding flow of the Mississippi River was straightened. Betty told us, "Once, so the story goes, the lake was populated by pirates who would hide in its unseen bends to jump on unsuspecting river travelers." Now there was no pirate that we could see, only a beautiful lake with magnificent bald cedars hugging the shores and masking the segregation between the black and the white communities.

It was in the white community where the private academy stood, established in the late 1960s when the formerly all-white high school became the "integrated public school." At that time, more than 90% of white families removed their children from the integrated school and sent them to the private academy. The two school districts still existed side by side in 1989 even though many white parents could hardly afford both taxes for the public school and tuition for the academy. Neither district had adequate numbers of teachers, sufficient curriculum materials, or specialists for the handicapped or gifted. The two school systems, side by side in the same community, were testaments to an economically bereft public system and a spiritually bereft private system. Under those economic conditions, no one was winning, and those whom we interviewed were not happy with the status quo.

Here was Betty Robinson, however, steadfast and determined to make a difference for the young people of her community. "There's this sense I have," she told us, "that I'm going to have a chance to straighten it all out. I know they need me here. It's a real challenge to help these kids. I want to make the big difference for at least a few of them."

As we talked with Betty in the hallway outside her classroom, a small and smiling girl approached us. It was Betty's youngest sister, the 13th Robinson child and a fifth grader at Booker T. Washington. Betty hugged her, then introduced us to her. We felt uplifted by Betty's spirit and the happy glow in her little sister's eyes. At the same time, we felt depressed and overwhelmed by the herculean professional challenge that Betty had undertaken.

### Gary and Karen Ritter

After leaving Betty, we zigzagged north up the Mississippi River, stopping to visit districts in Mississippi, Tennessee, and Arkansas. Toward the end of March, we arrived at a small district in Northeast Missouri. There we met Gary and Karen Ritter.

The stairs creaked and the building groaned as we climbed to the second floor of an ancient senior high, constructed in 1916. Hunched over a desk with reading glasses perched precariously on the bridge of his nose was Gary Ritter, a lanky man of medium build, expecting our visit to his senior literature class. He greeted us warmly and invited us to sit anywhere in the room. We sat in the back just to the side of a visiting parent, who apparently also was interested in observing Mr. Ritter's class.

After briefly introducing the 3 of us to the 15 students, Gary started, "Today we are discussing the short story by Ann Beattie,

'Imagine a Day at the End of Your Life.' What's it about?" After a long, silent pause, one student offered, "About an old man's strange ways at the end of his life." Ritter accepted that by saying, "OK, that's one way to look at it; anyone else?" "Yes," another student exclaimed, "I think it's about how hard it is to be yourself." "Yes," Gary said quickly, "what gave you that idea?" "Well, it's how he's trying to find his place in nature." "OK, good," said Ritter, "anyone else?" A third student said nervously, "I don't like his wife and daughters; they are mean." Ritter asked that student, "What happens in the story that gives you those feelings?" "I don't know," the student responded. Ritter waited, looked down at his book, then looked up again at the same student and waited. The student finally said, "They don't include him in their conversations." "Yes, I see that too," said Ritter.

"Let's look at how the story starts," Ritter suggested. "The first line is powerful—often the first sentence is very important in short stories. What does it say? Helen, please read it aloud for us." She did; and Ritter said that the key clause was, "he felt subsumed by them." Then: "What does 'subsume' mean . . . anyone?" There was no answer. "Let's look it up in the big dictionary!" Ritter moved to a table near the windows and picked up *The Random House Dictionary of the American Language*. He handed it to Mary. She looked up *subsume*. "It's on page 1418. It has three definitions," she said. Mary read from the dictionary, "to take up into a more inclusive classification."

"Yes, good Mary, that's an appropriate definition of subsume for this story. Tell us why John." John kept silent for a few seconds; then he said, "The man believes that his wife and two daughters have classified him." "Yes, good John, what sort of a classification might it be?" "Oh," John whispered, "maybe of any old man." "Yes," Ritter proclaimed, "yes, I believe we are beginning to understand how the man in Beattie's story feels."

All in the room, even the visiting parent and the two of us, were on the edge of our seats. The students had become thoroughly engaged with Ritter and one another in examining the story and in putting themselves into the shoes of the old man. Ritter did not tell them what the story said or what Beattie had in mind. He was skillfully stimulating the students to think and to build upon one another's ideas. Ritter led the class through the story, carefully choosing a sentence, word, or image on which to focus. We listened, thoroughly absorbed ourselves, to students talking to one another about how the man finds his individuality at last through his painstaking examination of the trees, plants, and birds that had surrounded him his whole life.

"Have you felt subsumed?" Ritter asked. "yes," one student immediately responded. A few others nodded their heads up and down. "How?" No one spoke. Ritter shouted, "As teenagers?" There was a chorus of "Yes!" "How else?" Students then called out in rapid fire: "As small-town kids" . . . "As farmers" . . . "As country bumpkins" . . . "As students" . . . "As boys" . . . "As girls."

"Yes," Ritter responded, "we are each of us classified into categories by others. I feel subsumed, too—as a teacher, a husband, a father. Perhaps, Ann Beattie, herself, feels that way, too. Perhaps for her, it's being classified as a woman, as a writer, or as a female writer. Let's think more about how we subsume one another before our next class." As we left the classroom, we reflected on Buber's distinction between I-Thou and I-It.

Gary Ritter had a preparation period later that day, so we went to chat with him at that time. He had been teaching literature in this district for 12 years. He was striving to make lifelong readers out of his students. He didn't know how well he was succeeding. Some favorite writings he assigned were *To Kill a Mockingbird, Catcher in the Rye, All My Sons,* and *The Miracle Worker.* He preferred literature that would help his students to probe their own lives and to get them to appreciate the lives of others.

"I have a fundamental belief in reading," he said. "I believe that I do make readers out of a few of them, but there's a real downside to teaching here." Ritter went on to tell us about his lack of voice in influencing the school administration, the very high value put on football and basketball by his fellow educators and the community, and the increased numbers of families with psychological problems. He was also frustrated by the failures of some of his best students during their first year at college.

As we interviewed Gary, his wife, Karen, arrived at the doorway. She stood about five feet two inches with a medium build. She wore a metal brace on her left leg, a legacy of childhood polio. Karen's classroom was only a few doors down and across the hall from Gary's. She taught composition and drama, and explained that she frequently used her metal brace and handicap as a "starting point for discussions about differences between people." "I love teaching," she told us, "but I wouldn't be doing it right now if it weren't for the money."

Karen went on to tell about their two young children and how she would rather be staying home with the younger one now "until he's ready for school." She was frustrated and "felt guilty" about giving him over to a baby-sitter every day, but they "simply could not make ends meet without the two salaries." Their expenses had nearly doubled a few years ago when they decided to move out of town to obtain more privacy. That move meant higher mortgage payments, increased taxes, and higher car expenses.

"Sure, I touch a few lives here in my teaching," she told us, "and so I get satisfaction out of teaching. But there is a lot of frustration, too. I used to direct a school play once a year and now there's no financial support for it. The only entertainment that counts in this district is football. I used to have more time to grade papers, but we had to let go of an English teacher two years ago and still don't have the funds to hire her back. I would like to take off for a few years to be with my son, but we're afraid they won't hire me back. So we feel stuck in what we are doing and mostly unappreciated."

We ended our frank conversation with the depressed Ritters by commenting about how impressed we were with Gary's skillful teaching of the Ann Beattie story. Gary brightened up and smiled with appreciation, telling us, "I never receive support from my administrators, colleagues, or parents about my teaching." With a bittersweet smile and sardonic twinkle in his eye, he said, "It's easy to feel subsumed here—subsumed into an inferior category."

## Peter Olsen

We spent 70 days of our 160-day trip traveling near the great 2,000-mile liquid highway of middle America, the Mississippi River. We sat on a bench on Beale Street in Memphis, camped near the Tom

Sawyer cave in Hannibal, hiked through the Native American settlements at La Crosse, and walked to the great river's source at Lake Itasca in Northern Minnesota, where snow flurries greeted the early spring. We visited Betty Robinson not far from the mouth of the Mississippi River, the Ritters halfway up it, and Peter Olsen not far from its source.

It was finally spring or, more accurately, barely spring when we met Peter Olsen in a small district in Northwestern Minnesota. Before meeting him, we were in a blue funk over the economic poverty of the small districts we had visited along the Mississippi. In one district, teachers with as many as 12 years' teaching experience were being let go. The English department in one high school had dwindled in one year from seven to five teachers, resulting in the elimination of advanced courses in composition, drama, and English literature. In another district, the high school teachers had cut in half the numbers of writing assignments for students to cope with their heavy burdens of correcting and grading. At the same time, speech and drama had been dropped from the curriculum. And then we met Peter Olsen, a man in his late twenties, medium height and youthful in appearance and style, who, with childlike enthusiasm and a breath of fresh, May air, was teaching students how to read drama and act in serious theater.

"I really didn't know what to major in when I went to college," Olsen confided in us. "I didn't even know what I was doing in college. I came from a poor farm family with very little encouragement to go to college. I was fortunate to have had a really good English teacher in high school, and since I liked to read, I decided to major in English. I figured I could always read what was assigned and 'bullshit' my way through on the papers and the essay exams. Yes, I decided early in college that I wanted to teach English. My adviser told me that I'd also need a minor, which I would be prepared to teach, so I went to the college yearbooks to find out what English majors chose for their minors. Most of them chose speech, so I decided I would too. Later, I discovered that a requirement in speech was to take at least one course in acting. So I did and I got hooked. One thing led to another and by my senior year I never wanted to leave the theater, even to eat or sleep. Drama became my baby!"

Olsen loved to take ill-at-ease adolescents and transform them into "fair gentlemen and ladies" much "like Professor Higgins did," he told us, in *My Fair Lady.* "After all," he said, "you know that Ibsen, himself, grew up in an uptight, conservative environment much like the one in this town. What are you going to do with one month of summer and 11 months of tough sledding, whether it's Minnesota or Norway? Well, here [put on a play] is what you do. My students like to imagine themselves in another place, at another time. It frees them up. They get a real look at life that way."

Olsen told us that he did not have his students read a lot of plays. Rather, he preferred to go deeply into only a few. His favorites were *Hedda Gabler* ("I played in it twice in college; I guess that's why I like it so much"), *Death of a Salesman* ("There's so much right with that play that's wrong about America"), and *King Lear* ("Most of these kids have grandparents about to die"). He thought that most English teachers were trying to cover too much with their students and that the "students get so stuffed that they lose their appetite for reading good literature." He would rather do a few things right so that "the material will make an imprint on their minds."

Like virtually all other teachers in small districts, Olsen was frustrated and angered over the lack of strong support at home for the academic program at school. "I get mad," he said, "not with what the kids do—even when they screw off now and then—but with the narrow-minded attitude of the unthinking adults around here." He complained to us about "the small-world view" and about "the lack of appreciation for good theater," but he was pleased with his students and looking forward to their performance of *Hedda Gabler.* "Ibsen would be proud of us," he said. "He, too, had to put up with tight-minded, hard asses in turn-of-the-century Norway, and we aren't far from that here. We'll work on it for another four weeks before we perform it. It will be good!"

On the wall behind his desk, Peter Olsen had a poster that read, "If you demand excellence, you'll get it."

## SOCIAL CONDITIONS OF TEACHING

We were overwhelmed by the pall of poverty that covered many of the small districts in which the teachers worked. The signs of economic austerity were as apparent to us as they were to the Joads on their trek from Oklahoma to California. Unfortunately, when we searched the minds and hearts of the teachers to understand their professional lives within the small districts, we found an even bleaker and depressing reality. Most of them, some 95 out of 119, believed that their teaching job had become more arduous compared with a decade ago, particularly because of the increased numbers of families in their small districts who were not supporting the school's curriculum at home. Teachers spoke frequently about students who missed school for reasons other than sickness and students who did not complete homework on time. The stories they told about dysfunctional family dynamics and low parental concern for academic matters sounded similar to teachers' stories we've heard in urban schools.

Hard economic conditions also were having a direct effect on the school's curriculum, particularly in English, foreign language, and science. High school English teachers, whom we systematically interviewed in all 25 districts, complained bitterly of the strong pressures they were feeling from their administrators to assign more writing projects to students, even in the face of declining numbers of English teachers and insufficient curriculum materials. In eight districts, teachers were expected to meet six classes a day in composition and felt frustrated because they were unable to give adequate feedback to students on the quality of their writing. Most small districts could afford only one foreign language teacher; five districts were sharing their one foreign language teacher with other neighboring districts. Twelve districts were having difficulty keeping science teachers, who would teach for one or two years and then be drawn off to a more lucrative job with less class preparation in a metropolitan area.

And, within the professional staffs themselves, there were frequently occurring misunderstandings between teachers and administrators: 60% of teachers complained about the lack of supportive communication with their administrators. Nearly 80% of teachers felt frustrated over having too little influence on administrative decisions in their districts. That 80% figure is considerably higher than the results of a study by the Carnegie Foundation (1988) in which a survey of more than 22,000 teachers nationwide showed that

37% were "not very involved in shaping the curriculum"; 51% had "not participated in formulating standards or in determining policy within their districts"; and 53% had "not been asked for input in creating rules for student behavior in the school." From their point of view, teachers in small districts were working harder than ever before, were under increased pressure to raise student achievement, faced a larger number of unsupportive families and reluctant students, and had less and less opportunity to influence their own administration on how the district and school should operate. Considering the many obstacles teachers faced, it may not be surprising that we did not see more inspired teaching or more I-Thou relationships in the classroom.

Despite these obstacles, 115 of the 119 teachers strongly preferred teaching in small districts and many were outspoken about their lack of desire to teach in larger suburban or urban districts. Of these teachers, 90% were born and raised in small towns; many had grown up, in fact, in the very town in which they were teaching. Many who had moved to the small district from cities did not wish to go back. Relaxed and confident, they felt safe and secure and did not want to live in a more crowded community. The majority liked that they knew almost everyone well, that they did not have to lock their cars or homes, and that their schools were free of drugs (though not alcohol). They also appreciated the fact that their high school was the social and entertainment center of the community and that they were an integral part of a community nexus, giving them an identity and secure place in an increasingly troubled and fragmented urban world.

## TEACHERS' AMBIVALENT FEELINGS

Most teachers liked teaching in a small district, at least in some ways. They would say to us, "I know everyone so when a kid is in trouble, chances are I know the brothers or sisters, and I can help." "The quality of life is good here on my salary." "I don't have to deal with traffic or crowds." "It's neighborly; people really help each other." "My roots are here; this is where I was raised and this is where I want to raise my kids."

Yet the sweet taste of teaching in small districts was tempered by bitterness. With each pleasant occurrence, there arose an equally powerful disadvantage. A common metaphor that came up again and again in our conversations with both students and teachers was that of "the big fish in a small pond." Feelings of superiority in local academic and extracurricular activities gave way to contrasting feelings of inferiority and self-doubt as the students and teachers ventured forth into the larger society. A teacher's exhilaration with helping students achieve during their senior high years too frequently gave way to the discouragement and frustration of meeting students who were returning home emotionally wrung out after less than a year away at the state university. Even the safety of a crime-free community, in which everyone knew everyone, was tempered by the teachers' claustrophobic feelings of being cornered, scrutinized, and judged by a gossiping public. As Karen Ritter so poignantly explained, "We moved ten miles out of this 'nice' town and almost doubled our expenses just to get some privacy."

Teachers' sense of noble service to the community clashed with their realization that what teachers do to help students learn was not being valued by townspeople. As one teacher put it in rural Mississippi, "Here you either own the land, or you work for someone who owns the land, or you teach." What was cherished in the small towns we visited was holding property or the traditional status attached to the family's long years of residence there.

In many places, teachers were the only remaining professionals in the region, because, as the economy had declined during the 1980s, the professionals—the doctors, dentists, and lawyers—had moved to greener pastures. In one district, a teachers' strike—the first in local history—occurred because the self-employed board members could not understand why the teachers should get increased retirement benefits. One board member told us, "Why shouldn't they live off social security too, just like us?" One frustrated teacher reported, "My wife drives 50 miles to go shopping, because with the strike it's too uncomfortable for her to shop at our local store." Obviously, the idyllic small town has its downside.

## DEDICATION, FRUSTRATION, AND HOPE:
## INGREDIENTS FOR CHANGE

Like Steinbeck's Joad family, the teachers we met were full of dedication, frustration, and hope. We spoke with 61 elementary, 16 middle school, 11 junior high, and 31 senior high teachers; 87 were women and 32 were men. The teachers in elementary school, most of them female, ranged in age from 26 to 55; 90% had grown up in small towns, and all but 3 had married people also from small towns. Only one of the elementary teachers was thinking of moving away from the district in which she was working. And 60% were still taking courses and workshops to expand their competencies, even though they had to travel long distances to the local university or to educational conferences.

The secondary teachers ranged in age from 24 to 58; 92% percent had grown up in small towns; 20% had attended the very school in which they were teaching. More secondary than elementary teachers spoke, regardless of age, about their plans for retirement. Although a few teachers in the North who spoke of retirement mentioned living in the South for part of the year, no teacher expected to retire away from the small town in which he or she currently lived. In essence, the teachers we interviewed were decidedly local and antiurban in their preferences for living arrangements. Those who had taught for more than 15 years in the small district often had some acreage on which they were growing crops or grazing animals. Their low salaries as teachers were being supplemented by a modest second income from farming.

Regardless of sex or grade level, the teachers portrayed a mixture of dedication, frustration, and hope. Although elementary teachers spent more time enhancing the appearance of their classrooms and secondary teachers more time in extracurricular activities, all were dedicated to their students and to the values of small-town life. Of the secondary teachers we interviewed, 60% (we estimated 40% of teachers overall) regularly spent from two to four hours after school supervising students in extracurricular activities. One high school teacher in New Mexico told us, "Along with supervising the student council, I help coach girls' basketball and boys' track." A junior high teacher in Montana said, "We have an amazing number of student activities at this school. Yes, in Montana the schools really are the social centers. Every teacher has at least one extracurricular responsibility, and a few of us, like me, have two responsibilities." At a junior high in Oregon, we watched staff members listing all of the social activities, other than sports and intramurals, that they had in their school. The list of 78 activities covered two pieces of poster paper; the number of activities exceeded the number of staff members in the school.

In one way or another, 90% of the elementary and 70% of the secondary teachers told us how much they cared about the academic *and* the social development of the students. "You know," one fourth-grade teacher in Arizona told us, "with the way families are breaking up, we have to be concerned with a lot more than the 3 Rs. We've got to help our students learn how to cope, to adjust, and to relate well with others." An experienced junior high teacher in Texas said, "This age has always been tough to manage, but over the last few years, it's gotten even tougher. We have to be teachers and counselors at the same time. I go out of my way to make sure kids are comfortable with one another and with me while they are learning the science that I teach." A California high school teacher said, "Sure, I want them to know how to read and to write, but I'm just as interested in their developing some self-confidence and esteem."

Further, 80% of teachers spoke about the various ways they were trying to improve themselves; 90% were spending their own money to purchase books and materials needed in their classrooms; and 100% were troubled by students who were not performing well in school. Those indicators of dedication to teaching and to students were surpassed only by the many frustrations they felt about their social conditions. Inequitable state funding, antiquated industries, and disappearing small farms were dramatically changing the idyllic picture of many small towns, especially those that had formerly relied on a single economic source.

Because of depressing economic times during the 1980s, schools in small districts all over America were undergoing a continuous drain on their resources, both physical and human. Their decaying buildings were barely adequate, new books and educational materials were not being purchased, new teachers with fresh ideas were not being hired, and experienced teachers were overloaded with teaching, counseling, committee work, and extracurricular activities. On top of that, many families were caving in because of unemployment or underemployment, and the stress of poverty was bringing on drinking, spouse beating, child abuse, and divorce.

Teachers were becoming increasingly frustrated with the lack of school support at home. Fifteen elementary teachers complained about the lack of parental initiative in seeing that their children were getting homework done. Seventeen secondary teachers complained about the lack of parental effectiveness in controlling the misbehavior of their children in school. A junior high teacher in Michigan summarized this frustration when she said, "99% of kid problems in school come from parent problems at home." A high school science teacher in Arkansas blurted in frustration, "Teachers are being blamed for parent problems!"

During the 1980s, just as the economic decline accelerated in small districts, the clamor throughout the nation for increased student achievement also accelerated. We saw six teachers, in as many districts and states, reluctantly succumbing to the pressure to raise student achievement by teaching to the test. They were coaching their students on how to take tests, how best to guess when they weren't sure, and what to look for in the test. We saw four teachers using item-by-item results from last year's test to guide them in preparing the students for this year's test.

Teachers' frustrations centered primarily on students who were not achieving and the lack of help and encouragement that those students were experiencing at home. They were frustrated by the absence of new texts and by insufficient educational materials. They were frustrated, too, that their own administrators were avidly passing on to them the pressures for change from the state departments of education. Nowhere were frustrations with "pressure-packed" administrators stronger than in Texas and Tennessee. Teachers everywhere, however, spoke about "communication problems" with their administrators. They did not believe that, even with small-district size in their favor, their superintendents were accessible to them, nor did they think that their anxiety and frustration were being heeded by their principals.

As the teachers told their stories, touched with dedication, anger, despair, and hope, we kept wondering, why do they stay? Why don't they find a district that will support and endorse their efforts, that will respect the contributions they can make to students? Mobility is as American as cherry pie. We, ourselves, as mobile Americans, had followed university jobs from Michigan to Pennsylvania to Oregon. Why do these teachers stay in small-town districts?

## BELONGING: THE QUEST FOR COMMUNITY

When Tocqueville got on the ship in Brooklyn harbor to return to France after his year-long visit to the United States, he had enough notes to write a monograph on American prisons (his primary task) and two large volumes on American culture. Among the many vivid impressions he took from his grand tour from Boston to Sault Sainte Marie to New Orleans and back to New York was that we are a "nation of joiners." Tocqueville thought of our brand of individualism as a sort of "group individualism"; he saw Americans searching for peer associations and belonging. What Tocqueville saw more than 150 years ago lives on today, we think, particularly among the teachers in small districts.

As we pored over our own high pile of interview notes and reflected on the teachers we could so vividly conjure up, Tocqueville's theme of "American belonging" kept repeating itself. It reverberated through our thoughts not only about teachers but also about the students and administrators we had met. The word *belong* kept coming up. For example, we remembered talking with a young man, a senior in a small school in rural Mississippi. He was planning to go to college, to become a teacher and coach, and to return to this same high school. "This is where I belong, so I will return." Marie, a young elementary teacher in Louisiana, said, "I tried to move away. I went to Baton Rouge for three years. You'd think people would be the same everywhere but Baton Rouge was foreign to me. They don't know the meaning of being Southern. So I came home. I like it here. I've lived here since I was 4, I like the lake, I like the land, I like the country. I belong here."

Indeed, the word *belong* recurred often in our conversations. Susan, a teacher in Texas, used the word. She went to college, married, moved to Austin, divorced, and came "home." "My father lived on the original acreage from 1871; this is where I belong." Robert, a teacher in North Dakota, also used the word. He went to college, then the army, and came back home to teach and to run the family farm. "My great-grandfather came here in 1878. There wasn't much around here, but he and his wife stuck it out. This is our family farm, and I'm the first-born son. I belong here and intend to stay."

What these teachers were reporting was not just love for a physical place; it also had to do with their deep need for long-term, close, and personal relationships. As urban individuals, they would feel alone, cut off from the community and their roots. In their small-scale environments, they had developed a sense of community. They simply assumed that they would have peer associations with familiar people in schools, churches, and taverns. They did not have to search for community; it was there, it was given.

Durkheim's word *anomie* reflected much of what our interviewees thought was present in urban, depersonalized society. They saw themselves striving to avoid the detached, anonymous, and disconnected lives of people in urban settings. They would have appreciated George Herbert Mead's ideas about community published in 1934 (pp. 270-271):

We have not taken very seriously our membership in the human society but it is becoming more real to us. . . . The question whether we belong to a larger community is answered in terms of whether our own action calls out a response in this wider community, and whether its response is reflected back into our own conduct.

The teachers believed that their actions could call out a response from others more readily in a town of 4,000 than in a city of 4 million, more effectively in a district of 2,000 students than one of 20,000 or 200,000.

Phil, a high school counselor in Arizona, a vivacious man with a lilting voice revealing his Hispanic heritage, had returned to his small-town home near a copper mine "to clean it up." He told us, "The kids were out of control, the community was torn apart, and I could do something." Phil was proud of his accomplishments in procuring college scholarships for many of his high school students. "In this district," Phil said, "one can belong and make a difference." As Betty Robinson told us, "There's this sense I have that I'm going to have a chance to straighten it all out. I know they need me here." Their words reminded us of Holden Caulfield's wish in *Catcher in the Rye* to keep little children from falling off a cliff.

As we drove west across the northern tier of states and got closer and closer to our Oregon home, our own place of belonging, we kept reflecting on the teachers we had interviewed. Had they managed to escape the downside of American urban life? We wondered. Had they sidestepped the modern error of dividing life into the separate functional spheres of home, workplace, and leisure? We weren't certain, because we could not rid ourselves of the hunch that small-district teachers were paying a price for working there. They were under public scrutiny, for example. They were a part of a fragile fabric, which, if torn, as we thought it was torn in many places, would make life very unhappy for them. A torn fabric, like a run in a nylon stocking, can be clearly seen by most people in a small community. And the tear of misunderstanding was certainly visible in many of the districts we visited.

We must report, however, what we saw as well as what we intuited. Even though stories of frustration and anger poured from the teachers' hearts, we were impressed, over and over, with how much hope so many of them articulated about their schools and their students. Most believed that small-town America would prevail and that small districts would turn out to be more effective than large districts. Most believed that rural America would rebound from its economic malaise and again become prosperous and creative. More than half of the teachers thought that in the 1990s urban citizens will seek to live in small towns and that new industries will inevitably develop in rural America.

More than half of the teachers believed that, with the automobile so available and the computer connections to communication centers so accessible, it will become feasible to carry on a small-town atmosphere while shopping and even working elsewhere. Most believed, also, that students in small districts will succeed in American society, even in the face of the increasing numbers of psychological casualties from broken homes. An elementary teacher in Iowa told us, "Most of these students feel good about themselves and their community. In the long run, they'll do just fine." A high school teacher in New Mexico remarked, "Eventually, the economy is going to turn around here. You'll see lots of people from the cities coming here soon."

Are they right? We think some changes will have to occur for teachers in small districts before the Joads and the Judy Landrys will return to them for a more connected and integrated life in the community. Here are some of our ideas.

## TARGETS OF CHANGE

The teachers of small districts, overall, gave too little attention, we think, to two important foci in their jobs: (a) They did not work together in formal ways to improve their instructional programs, nor did they even talk about doing so. We saw only 3 out of 80 staffs in which even a little consideration was being given to peer coaching and interdisciplinary teamwork. Although we witnessed griping and complaining among teachers, we did not see them meeting to solve academic problems or to make decisions about instruction. (b) They did not use participatory methods much in their classes. Mostly they talked to and at their students. We estimated that three quarters of the classroom talk we observed was teacher's talk and that three quarters of that was unidirectional lecturing. We saw only a few instances of genuine cooperative learning; they were in Judy Landry's school.

## *Teachers in Relation to Colleagues*

The most popular national figure in education for the teachers and administrators was Madeline Hunter. Her categories for analyzing teaching, as described in the ITIP (Instructional Theory Into Practice) model (Hunter, 1979), were being used widely, particularly by young principals ambitious to impress the superintendents and state departments of education with their skill at supervising teachers.

The typical execution of ITIP, however, would not have made Madeline Hunter very happy. Armed with a list of ITIP behaviors—such as stating instructional goals clearly, engaging students in behavioral practice, reinforcing correct answers, and so on—the principals were using Hunter's categories as a checklist for classroom observations. During their visits to the classroom, the principals expected to see behaviors reflecting of the ITIP categories being carried out by the teacher. In effect, the principal would rate the teacher's performance according to how thoroughly the categories of ITIP were implemented.

That style of supervision led many teachers to put on an act for the observing principal. As a fifth-grade teacher in Tennessee told us, "My principal knows what I *can* do from his ITIP observations, but he doesn't know what I *do* do!" Madeline Hunter (1986) herself has complained about the distorted adaptation of her theories. She has had two concerns. First, she worried that a narrow application of ITIP would encourage teachers to use only direct, didactic instruction instead of also using discovery, inquiry, and problem-solving methods. Second, she was concerned that a supervisor's use of her categories for teacher evaluation would relegate ITIP to the narrow context of making personnel decisions about probationary teachers rather than as a catalyst for school improvement. She argued that the ITIP model should afford the categories for collegial collaboration. In school after school, we found evidence that Hunter's hopes for ITIP were not being realized.

Advocates of site-based management of schools, such as White (1989) and Sarason (1990), believe that students will be better served by teachers who collaborate in school improvement efforts. They argue also that increased authority for teachers in the school will improve teacher morale and staff climate. We believe that site-based management could make a difference to the academic excellence of the school if the teachers, themselves, rather than the administrators, become responsible for monitoring one another's instruction.

At least three kinds of collegial collaboration should be tried: *sharing, coaching,* and *consultation.* Peer sharing consists of teachers giving one another information about curriculum, diagnostic insights into students, and instructional materials. We were impressed by the fact that more than 60% of the teachers were continuing to take courses and workshops even though a majority of those teachers were at the top of the salary schedule. We were discouraged, however, by the absence of communication among the teachers about what they were learning.

*Peer coaching* consists of collegial relationships in which teachers are expected to be experts in a system of thought, such as ITIP, guiding colleagues toward the adoption or refinement of some specific behavioral skills. Coaching implies judging and assisting another's capability in executing particular skills in the classroom. *Peer consultation* focuses on establishing collaborative working relationships among teachers so that all participants become more self-analytic and reflective about their own instructional strategies and skills.

Smith and Acheson (1991) offer a useful taxonomy and description of various forms of collaboration among teachers for instructional improvement. Among the types are the following: (a) In peer coaching with a focus on *Hunter's ITIP categories,* teachers pair, after attending in-service training sessions in ITIP, to learn to apply Hunter's system in their teaching. (b) In peer coaching on skills of *teaching effectiveness,* the focus is on bridging the gaps between what the teacher effectiveness research is saying and what happens in the classroom. Teachers work together, either in pairs or small grade-level or subject matter teams, to review effectiveness research that is appropriate to them and to observe one another applying it in the classroom. (c) In peer coaching on *different models of teaching,* small groups of teachers study the seven models of teaching delineated by Joyce and Weil (1980) and then observe one another applying them in the classroom. (d) With peer consultation for *fine-tuning and reflection,* in contrast to coaching, this type of collegial collaboration stresses personal growth through the mind of the teacher and is designed to offer opportunities for the refinement of one's teaching. (e) Peer consultation for *reflective practice and innovation* emphasizes collaborative activities such as action-research theory building and reflection by writing professional diaries and reading about one another's thoughts. For more details, see the March 1991 ("The Reflective Educator") issue of *Educational Leadership.* (f) In peer consultation *and organization development,* the focus is on developing trusting relationships between teachers so that they can be comfortable and productive in group problem solving and collaborative decision making about academic problems and challenges. Organization development for teams of teachers, as described by Schmuck and Runkel (1988), aims to foster healthy communication among teachers so that they will feel secure and supported in trying instructional innovations.


## *Teachers in Relation to Students*

Berliner (1983) demonstrated how teacher-student relationships can be analyzed according to the *activity structures* that teachers use. Activity structures such as reading circles, mediated presentations, seat work in rows, lecturing, group discussion, and working in pairs call for different teacher behaviors and different classroom norms to guide the behavior of students in the structure. We observed a poverty of alternative activity structures in the high school classes.

In contrast, kindergartens, full of color and variety, had multiple learning centers with lofts, tents, sandboxes, fishbowls, animal cages, art centers, and other nooks and crannies of fascination. On our gray days, frustrated with our observations of teachers' complaining and administrators' insensitivity, we sought to visit a kindergarten to lift our spirits.

"Discover children in this school; you'll see how much like play some work can be" was written above a kindergarten room in the Upper Peninsula of Michigan, and we wished it had been the philosophy at other grades in that same district. Kindergarten students were curious, active, bright-eyed, and smiling. The teachers, in all instances women, were relaxed, complimentary, active, smiling, and caring.

Other grade levels could benefit from employing a greater variety of appropriate activity structures. Berliner recommends, and we concur, that teachers set aside time to establish rules of behavior for each prominent activity structure they will use. In reading circles, for example, students would be obliged to raise their hands when they want help. Or all media-aided presentations could be followed by small discussion groups during which students discuss what they learned from the presentation. During group discussion, the teacher would try to paraphrase each student's remark before responding to it. Teachers might develop lists of rules for each activity structure early in the year and have the class review them once a month.

We expected to find many more activity structures in the classroom of small districts than we did. In particular, we expected to see more than the five instances of cooperative learning groups we did see. Current literature is replete with example after example of alternative forms of cooperative learning. The evaluative research on cooperative learning, both for academic achievement and for enhanced social support in classroom peer relations, has been very supportive. (For details, see Schmuck & Schmuck, 1992.) Apparently, most of the teachers we visited did not see the literature, nor were they receiving information about it in their in-service training sessions.

We are particularly fond of the innovative work on cooperative learning of the Sharans in Israel. Yael and Shlomo Sharan (1992), having been influenced by Dewey's (1922) project method and by Sarason's (1990) concern about empowering both teachers and students, have developed the "Group Investigation Method." With it, teachers can successfully alter classroom norms toward increased cooperation while simultaneously enhancing student learning and achievement. The instructional tasks can focus on a variety of things, such as a social problem, a famous person's life, a historical period, a book, or a scientific problem. All activities by the students take place as part of collective effort. Every learning activity requires group decision, and thus constant coordination among participants is required to carry out the task.

In planning and carrying out the Group Investigation Method, students are led through a series of six consecutive stages. Stage 1 consists of specifying the task and organizing students into investigation teams. Typically, the teacher presents a general area of study, encouraging the students to suggest specific topics for study. After discussion, the students select topics and join investigation teams. Stage 2 is planning the learning task. The teams determine what to study, how to study, and the purpose of the study. Stage 3 consists of carrying out the investigation, and Stage 4 consists of preparing a final report. Stage 5 consists of presenting the report to the rest of the class, and Stage 6 entails a cooperative evaluation of each of the investigations by all students and the teacher.

In a field experiment in Israel, Sharan and Shacher (1986) compared students who used the method in social studies and geography with students taught by a traditional whole-class, lecture and recitation method—the kind we saw all along the blue highways of America. They found not only that there was much more cooperative give-and-take between students of different ethnic groups in the cooperative discussions but also that the achievement levels of the students who worked cooperatively were higher than those of the students taught in the traditional manner. Sharan and Shacher also demonstrated that Middle Eastern students, a minority ethnic group in Israel, gained even more from the cooperative investigations than the Western students. We believe, too, in the American context, that the Hispanic students of Arizona, California, and Texas could make significant achievement gains if encouraged to cooperate and to help one another in academic learning.

Teachers can reduce students' boredom with academic learning by engaging the students more in captivating interaction in the classroom. One route is to create a variety of activity structures so students maintain an interest in what is happening. Another route is to employ pairs, trios, and teams of four, five, or six in cooperative learning. A third route is to supplement academic instruction with a genuine concern for the students' thoughts and feelings about school and with the application of what is being learned to the community.

We met a senior high teacher in Idaho who was teaching her social studies students to shift between three cultures in the class. As she explained the cultures, the first is *a personal culture,* where we present our own personal thoughts, feelings, and values about the topic we are studying. She taught the students that an important guideline in the personal culture is respect and appreciation of differences, and an important verbal reaction is "I think . . ." or "I feel . . ." or "I value . . .." The second is *an academic culture,* where we study the ideas, research, and practices of experts. In this culture, students must learn how to move out of themselves to listen and to read carefully the complex ideas of others. Relevant guidelines for behavior are curiosity, hard study, and trying to commit information to memory. The third is *an application culture,* where we find out about problems in our community or school and seek to use information we have about ourselves and have learned from the experts to find solutions to those problems. Relevant guidelines for behavior are collaborative problem solving, trial and error, and evaluation of effects.

That teacher told us about a program that had influenced her thinking about the application culture. "In Atlanta, Georgia," she said, "high school students were required to take a course called 'Duties to the Community.' " We liked the idea and asked her to tell us more about it. "Well," she said, "I believe that in Atlanta the course consists of about 75 hours of unpaid volunteer service in community agencies under the supervision of teachers. The program aims to increase students' awareness of their civic responsibilities. Along with the hours of service, the students must write an essay or keep a diary that gets turned into the English teacher." She went on to tell us that she would be trying a similar course next year in her own school. We walked away thinking of how valuable a "Duties to the Community" course could be all over America.

The move beyond bittersweet belonging will start, we think, when teachers rededicate themselves to I-Thou relationships with their colleagues and students, convert their frustrations with their administrators into peer sharing, coaching, and consulting, and create a larger variety of "classroom happenings" with their students, including a mission for community improvement. Excitement and enthusiasm can be brought back to boring classrooms by coupling the academic life with personal and community interests.

## REFERENCES

Berliner, D. C. (1983). Developing conceptions of classroom environments: Some light on the T in classroom studies of ATI. *Educational Psychologist, 18*(1), 1-13.

Carnegie Foundation for the Advancement of Teaching. (1988). *Teacher involvement in decisionmaking: A state-by-state profile.* Washington, DC.

Dewey, J. (1922). *Human nature and conduct.* New York: Henry Holt. (See the selection reprinted in R. Archambault, Ed., *John Dewey on education: Selected writings,* Chicago: University of Chicago Press, 1964.)

Hunter, M. (1979). *Theory into practice.* El Segundo, CA: TLP Publications.

Hunter, M. (1986). Comments on the Napa County, California Follow-Through Project. *Elementary School Journal, 87*(2), 173-179.

Joyce, B., & Weil, M. (1980). *Models of teaching.* Englewood Cliffs, NJ: Prentice-Hall.

Mead, G. H. (1934). *Mind, self, and society* (C. M. Morris, Ed.; posthumously published). Chicago: University of Chicago Press.

The reflective educator. (1991, March) [Entire issue]. *Educational Leadership, 48*(6).

Sarason, S. (1990). *The predictable failure of educational reform.* San Francisco: Jossey-Bass.

Schmuck, R. A., & Runkel, P. J. (1988). *The handbook of organization development in schools* (3rd ed.). Prospect Heights, IL: Waveland.

Schmuck, R. A., & Schmuck, P. A. (1992). *Group processes in the classroom* (6th ed.). Dubuque, IA: William C Brown.

Sharan, S., & Shacher, C. (1986). *Cooperative learning effects on students' academic achievement and verbal behavior in multi-ethnic junior high school classrooms in Israel.* Tel-Aviv: Tel-Aviv University, School of Education.

Sharan, Y., & Sharan, S. (1992). *Group investigation: Expanding cooperative learning.* Albany: State University of New York Press.

Smith, N. S., & Acheson, K. (1991, February). Peer consultation: An analysis of several types of programs. In *Oregon School Study Council Bulletin* (Vol. 34, No. 6). Eugene: Oregon School Study Council. (booklet)

Steinbeck, J. (1939). *The grapes of wrath.* New York: Viking.

Tocqueville, A. de (1945). *Democracy in America.* New York: Knopf.

White, P. (1989, September). School-based management: What does the research say? *NASSP Bulletin,* pp. 1-7.

# 4

## Principals

### MOVING TOWARD
### INSTRUCTIONAL LEADERSHIP

It is really impossible to write about the schools. Teachers and children, parents and administrators, critics and professors—all obstinately refuse to behave in that neat statistical manner which can validate a commentary. The damnable difficulty is that all those connected with schools insist on behaving like people. "All you have to tell me about a man is that he's human," said Mark Twain, "you can't say anything worse."

*—Mayer, 1961, pp. 425-426*

We conceived our tour of small districts during Christmas 1987, after reading Least Heat Moon's personal and poignant travelogue, *The Blue Highways: A Journey Into America.* We already knew that we would spend six weeks during fall 1988 in China's Hebei Province, had previously spent sabbaticals in Louvain, Madrid, and Paris, with several side trips north to Finland and south to Italy, and had already made a few professional trips to Australia, Canada, England, and Mexico. We decided then that, in our forthcoming sabbatical, January to June 1989, we would tour the United States not only to compensate for so much foreign travel but so that we could also take a firsthand look at small districts. Most of our research and consulting had been carried out in urban or suburban districts, which we thought we knew fairly well. Reading Least Heat Moon's reflections on American society inspired us to travel the back roads to see for ourselves whether small is beautiful in American education.

Our plan to combine research with travel was cherished and lauded by envious colleagues at Lewis and Clark and the University of Oregon when we announced it in the summer of 1988. "Wow!" one said, "a trip to a Chinese University and an RV tour of the States, both in one school year!" Another told us, "What a dream come true. You were inspired, you made plans, and now you're actually going to do it." A third colleague commented, "I'll bet a lot of us think about combining RV travel with academic research, but you two have the ingenuity and persistence to pull it off."

Those and other comments like them gave us pride in what we were attempting. We began to believe that we truly did have an ingenious plan; we did not imagine then, however, the frustrating difficulties in travel we would encounter. Half way through the tour, on a cold, gray day in Missouri, we questioned our dogged persistence and, by the time we returned home to Oregon, we vowed that we'd rather spend six months in a tent than drive the White Tortoise on the blue highways for another six days.

Our difficulties were with the vehicle itself. Our good friends, Jean and Don, rented their Tioga to us at a very good price. They weren't traveling any because Jean was hard at work writing a doctoral dissertation. In fact, they hadn't used the RV much for the past two years. The White Tortoise had been left standing in Jean and Don's driveway. Like inactive athletes beyond their prime, the White Tortoise's reasonably handsome exterior belied a host of mechanical aches and pains in its interior that, unbeknown to Jean, Don, and us, were to keep it from performing the way it once could in its youth. We became its caretakers just before it was ready for a nursing home.

The actual kind of mechanical problems might not seem excessive considering a six-month, 10,000-mile trip. We replaced the battery, starter, one brake liner and two brake drums, some electric wiring, a little plastic tubing, and four tires. You had to be there, however, to feel sympathy for us.

Early one Monday morning, for example, the temperature dropped in a few hours from 42°F to −6°F, a drop that was more precipitous than the steep decline of the Dow-Jones Industrial average on "Black Monday" just four months previously. The furnace, which never quite worked right, died, the plastic water pipe froze, the starter imploded, and we had to be towed out of 14 inches of snow to the service station. We asked the mechanic, "What happened to the starter?" He responded simply, "Old and cold!" We felt he could have been talking about us, and here we were only to New Mexico with 21 districts yet to go. But the kindness of people counterbalanced our difficulties with the vehicle. While our home underwent repair in the service station, a gracious school secretary provided us room and board.

Three weeks later, we crossed the Mississippi River at Vicksburg accompanied by the loud, flapping sound of two back tires losing their rubber casings. We were horrified to think of all the Louisiana miles we had covered with our steel belts grinding into the highway. Up the Mississippi, at Hannibal, we felt the brake pedal descend closer and closer to the floor before the Tortoise would completely stop. Later the next day, crossing over the bridge at Keokuk, Iowa, we completely lost the ability to brake the vehicle, and the dreaded red brake light went on. Under the red light, the dashboard of the Tortoise read, *BRAKE FAILURE*. Have you ever tried to stop an RV without brakes? Now, we understand better why there are runaway ramps for trucks. It was a brake liner that broke and we lost all brake fluid.

We applaud the service station attendants across the country; they were invariably helpful and courteous—but enough about the woes of traveling in the White Tortoise.

*     *     *

Just as our friends had romanticized and glorified our plan for the blue highways tour, so too had we idealized the work of the principal, particularly that of the elementary principal, in small districts. As two people committed to school improvement and academic excellence, we envision the elementary principalship to be the ideal job from which to initiate planned change.

At first glance, at least, it would appear idyllic to be the principal of a small-town elementary school. After all, who is admired and respected more by those delightful kindergartners than their idol, the principal? We imagine a walk down the hallway to be accompanied by greetings with hugs and students eager to show off their latest accomplishments.

Imagine it! With eight years of successful classroom teaching and two years of administrative certification courses under your belt, you take over a cozy little school set on a pastoral knoll of live oaks among quiet neighbors in well-kept homes with green lawns just a few blocks away from a quaint, downtown square dating back to the turn of the century.

Your competent staff of sixteen teachers, a secretary, a custodian, two cooks, and three aides operates like a close-knit family. The supportive superintendent visits you now and then to tell you what a splendid job you are doing. The helpful and pleasant parents, 90% of whom are actively engaged in the school, support the teachers' efforts and yours. The well-behaved students, secure in their families and in their community, work diligently on their assignments in school and at home. Their joyous laughter can be heard resounding through the school's clean and orderly hallways.

With such ideal portraits of small-district elementary schools in the backs of our minds, we sought to discover what principals' work lives were really like by talking with them and observing them in action across the United States. In a nutshell, the principals' working days were about as tranquil and rewarding as driving through St. Louis in the White Tortoise.

What we found were *not* idyllic pedagogical portraits of charming simplicity. Rather, we found principals meeting eruptions of troubles throughout the week. Watching and listening to them, we felt much the way we did when the starter imploded, the tire casings began flapping, and the brakes failed. Indeed, the most serious difficulties for elementary and secondary principals alike in small districts were *not* very different than the difficulties of their urban counterparts.

## THE PRINCIPALS WE STUDIED

We interviewed 84 principals and assistant principals, each for more than an hour, shadowed them for parts of two days, and observed most of them in meetings with their superintendents and teachers. We also interviewed teachers in each school, in part, about their perceptions of their principal's administrative style.

Our interviewees were 46 secondary principals (high school and middle school or junior high) and 38 elementary; 45 of secondary principals were males, only 1 of whom was black. The only woman principal at the secondary level was a vice-principal. The mean age of the secondary principals was 49, with a range from 37 to 65; 35 had been raised in the local area; only 7 were born out of state.

The sample of 38 elementary principals comprised 28 men and 10 women (including 2 female assistant principals and 1 female head teacher). Only two elementary principals were members of a minority; both were black men. The mean age of the male elementary principals was 48, and, for the women, it was 43; the age range of all the elementary principals was 35 to 64. Of the 38 principals, 23 of them had been raised in the local area; 9 (7 men and 2 women) had been born out of state.

Overall, the male principals, totaling 73, had served as school administrators for an average of 14 years, whereas the 11 women had been administrators for an average of only 6 years. Of these principals, 47 men, but no woman, had been coaches of athletic teams.

Only eight men and one woman had been principal of a previous school. Among the elementary principals, three men and one woman were simultaneously supervising more than one school staff.

Because of our research and consulting experiences in Detroit, Los Angeles, Philadelphia, Portland, and San Francisco, and because the literature of professional education tends to emphasize the complexities of being an urban or suburban principal, we wondered whether principals in small districts would experience their job differently. Would, for example, the principals of small, out-of-the-way districts face fewer challenges and less conflict and have simpler work lives than their urban and suburban counterparts? Would small-district principals have administrative styles different than their metropolitan counterparts?

## CHALLENGES THE PRINCIPALS FACE

Even though principals in small districts do not encounter some of the social problems posed by the urban environment such as hard drugs or crime on the school grounds, they do face a multitude of administrative difficulties. Everywhere we traveled, being a successful principal required a juggling act.

The principals must juggle the academic deficits and affective needs of students from dysfunctional families with the demands of the public crying out for higher student achievement. They must strive to control the alcohol use of the adolescents in communities where the use of alcohol is a way of life for many of the adults. From 18 of the 46 secondary principals we interviewed, we heard gruesome stories about fatal automobile accidents befalling high school students.

Furthermore, the principals must strive to upgrade the quality of classroom teaching in their schools while at the same time they try to soothe the battered egos of their teachers who, for their part, feel beleaguered by continuing state mandates for change, decreasing financial resources, and threatening allegations from reformers about their lack of professional competence. The principals must manage the school's meager resources efficiently while they soothe the anger of staff members who have not received a decent pay raise in years.

Listen to the ways some of the principals themselves see it.

## Challenge 1: Student Motivation, Current Realities

- "We just have a different student population these days. They don't get as much psychological support at home as they used to" (Texas).
- "It's really hard to deal with our students' use of alcohol when so many parents in this community drink excessively" (Montana).
- "Parents don't seem to care about their kids today. They don't care if the homework gets done or not. They aren't really on top of what their kids are doing, either academically or socially" (Tennessee).
- "We encourage parents to read aloud to their child, but some can't; their life is too dysfunctional, and they can't help their child" (Arizona).
- "We need to work on self-esteem of the students *and* of the parents. Unfortunately, quite a few adults in this town don't have much self-respect" (California).
- "We need to recognize the Native Americans more. These poor children are in a very vulnerable situation. We need to recognize their culture and give more respect to it. We need to get more Native American parents involved in school" (New Mexico).

The principals had to deal with families unable to adapt to a downwardly spiraling economy and families that were not helping their youngsters respond productively to the teachers' expectations. In districts in Arizona, New Mexico, Texas, Louisiana, Mississippi, and Tennessee, in particular, the special needs of minority students exacerbated the problems of low student achievement for the principals. As the achievement of white students had declined, the achievement scores of minority youngsters, particularly from grade five and up, had declined even more than those of the majority whites.

In our interviews, 54 of 84 principals focused on the changing attitudes and motivation of the student population toward school and self as the first challenge facing the small-district school. Even in the most fortunate towns of Montana and New Mexico, where the civic leaders had capitalized on the area's natural beauty to strengthen the economy through tourism and to attract wealthy patrons to buy vacation houses, many of the new students in those schools had unskilled and transient parents who served the tourist industry with low-paying jobs and often unstable lives.

Of these principals, 65 acknowledged that many of their students were "at risk"; they believed that, without early and constructive intervention such as Head Start or other preschool programs, those youngsters would become burdens to society. And 68 principals expressed compassion for the out-of-school lives faced by many of their students. One principal in Arizona summed it up: "School is the nicest part of the day for some of these kids."

## Challenge 2: Teacher Improvement, Current Realities

Here are some quotations from the principals about their frustrations in pursuing the improvement of teachers:

- "My largest challenge is correcting a teacher. Correcting them for minor things like making sure they are in the room on time is easy. There aren't many problems like that anyway. It's when they are not getting along with a student and you know it's a personality clash and it's the teacher's fault, like when you know there isn't a good feeling tone in the class because of the teacher" (Washington).
- "We can't attract young, fresh minds at this location. We take whatever we can get. This year we hired 16 noncertified people on emergency certificates" (Texas).
- "Teachers can be our worst enemies sometimes. It's hard to get rid of poor teachers; even during their probationary periods we can run into roadblocks" (Montana).

- "The legislature has come down too hard on teachers. It forced us to use a new teacher-appraisal system based on Madeline Hunter. The teachers don't have a good taste in their mouths about it. We have to go in unannounced three times and if they are on the career ladder their money is tied to my appraisal" (Tennessee).
- "Our teachers are overloaded. We need to reduce the pressure from the onslaught of new curriculum. I think teachers verge on burn-out. They are growing hungry and tired, even in this isolated little town" (North Dakota).

Improvement of teaching was the most heralded objective of the educational reform movement in the 1980s. The president of the United States, the secretary of education, governors, and legislators all pointed the finger of responsibility at teachers for the alleged poor quality of education in our classrooms. School districts nationwide were pressured to retain only the best teachers and to replace ineffective teachers with new, more capable and better trained neophytes. In most small districts we toured, however, the superintendents and principals were having an onerous time hiring and retaining good teachers. It was primarily people who themselves had been students in small, out-of-the-way districts who yearned to teach in them and who therefore would apply for the openings. Many effective neophytes who had not been raised locally would leave, unfortunately, after only a year or two for higher salaries in metropolitan districts.

During the 1980s, compared with the 1970s, the number of college students who majored in business and accounting tripled, whereas students majoring in education became fewer. Moreover, because of the expanding economies in the Sunbelt states, many education majors spurned the low salaries in teaching and sought better paying jobs in business firms. Education majors who wanted to obtain teaching positions were attracted to the suburbs and cities of the Sunbelt for reasonable salaries and desirable living conditions. Just as dentists, doctors, and lawyers fled from small-town America in the 1980s, so too did many of our most promising young teachers.

## Challenge 3: Effective Staff Involvement, Current Realities

In our interviews with teachers, we asked about their voice in schoolwide problem solving and decision making. As we wrote in Chapter 3, our data showed that the majority of teachers were dissatisfied with their principals' administrative styles. A case in point was Betty Ann Swisher, a high school English teacher in North Dakota. A large, middle-aged woman with a commanding presence, she told us of her family's historical roots in the community on the Plains, where she had lived all her life except when she went away to college.

We met Swisher after a faculty meeting during which Fred Jensen, the principal, had spoken for 45 minutes on various noneducational topics. We sat on the side of the large classroom. Virtually every male teacher sat in the back of the room, far away from Jensen. Female teachers sat more to the front or on the side near us. The seating pattern was haphazard except for the segregation of males and females. The only utterances from teachers during the meeting were a few questions for clarification.

As we walked out of the room and down the hallway to Swisher's room, she commented, "Running faculty meetings, as you can see, is not one of Mr. Jensen's sterling qualities. His meetings are terrible."

When the three of us entered Swisher's classroom, a few students were waiting to receive feedback and advice from her about a paper she had assigned to them. She motioned for us to sit at a table near the windows and talked with the students for a few minutes. She joked with them and gave them the advice about their papers that they seemed to be seeking. Then she joined us for "some relaxed conversation" as she called it.

Swisher had been teaching English for 24 years. She delighted in telling us about her classes, both the "regular ones" for sophomores and juniors and the advanced classes she was doing with college-bound seniors. Like Gary Ritter, she was using *To Kill a Mockingbird* and *The Miracle Worker*. She also described how she had managed to teach some of the more controversial books in this community, such as *Lord of the Flies, The Grapes of Wrath,* and *Brave New World.* She told us, "Even though there is an adamant right-wing fringe group in this town, I'm such an established member here that no one complains about what I teach."

Swisher took pride in her ability to communicate with most of the students in her classes. She told us, "I'm strong on discipline, but also I keep their interest in literature. They know I don't fool around with assignments and such, but they also know that we'll have a lot of fun and that I will be fair." She proudly showed us examples of student papers that had been written in her advanced composition class. "A few of my students," she said, "have won writing awards in state competitions."

Swisher told us that she loved teaching and that she felt good about her career but, when we asked, "What sort of influence or voice do you have concerning schoolwide matters?" Betty Ann's answer was typical of what we heard from teacher after teacher. "I don't want to be an administrator," she said. "I want to be a teacher, *but* everything in this school pretty much is a one-sided affair. Mr. Jensen has many good qualities as a person, but running meetings and getting staff to work together aren't two of them." The three of us chuckled out loud over the ineffective staff meeting we had just watched.

Swisher continued, "According to district policy, even according to North Dakota statute, we are supposed to have a curriculum committee for teacher input. I've been on the committee and it's a joke. It's merely the strong arm of the administration. We don't meet to talk. We don't meet to decide. Mr. Jensen does not listen and is not a very open communicator. Don't get me wrong, I'm a strong person and I say what I want to say, but I'm essentially ignored. Frankly, I think Mr. Jensen has a real problem with strong women, so I just do my thing in the classroom."

Although Swisher, like so many other teachers we interviewed, was pleased with her job and school, she lamented the fact that teachers were not collaborating with the administrators in running the district. "It could be so much better here," she said. We could not disagree with Swisher's sentiments, because by that time we had toured 20 small districts and had heard her story retold often.

We found the principals in small districts to be friendly, approachable, and affable. Of course, they were very busy and therefore did not have much time for informal chitchat. More than their metropolitan counterparts, they were typically highly visible figures in the community, and therefore they seemed to have very little private life that was separated from their role in the school. Often, they had been teachers on the very staff they were administering. Still, more often than not, the principals' pictures of themselves as communicative, collaborative, and democratic with their teachers were illusions. In actuality, staff involvement in running most schools was more fiction than fact.

## PRINCIPALS' ADMINISTRATIVE STYLES

Educators and scholars agree that the primary tasks of the principal are to *lead* and to *manage* to promote teacher effectiveness and student learning. Leading, which is the "people" part of administration, consists of inspiring teachers to do the very best they can in facilitating student learning. Managing, which is the institutional part of administration, entails activities, in relation to teaching and learning, such as planning, setting goals, solving problems, and evaluating. Whereas leadership concerns arousing, engaging, and satisfying the private yearnings of teachers, management focuses on giving teachers a clear sense of the school running efficiently and effectively. Both leadership and management require the principal to use communication skills.

Some communication skills help build trust, confidence, and respect in the staff, by the principal's articulating dreams and visions about the school's mission, creating in the teachers an urgency to act, and establishing for the staff a feeling of pulling together. Other communication skills consist of the principal's initiating collaborative planning, running effective meetings, coordinating cooperative problem solving, and monitoring follow-up on decisions that are being implemented.

We think that successful principals will communicate administrative leadership by articulating visions of the good school and by modeling openness to receiving feedback from teachers. We believe also that successful principals will exhibit communication skills by

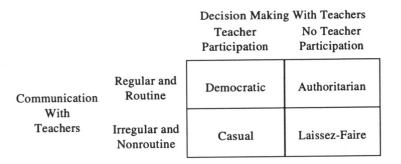

**Figure 4.1.** Leadership Styles of Principal

supporting routine data collection from the staff on how things are going and by fostering faculty discussions to encourage continual efforts to enhance teaching and learning.

Through our interviews and observations, we looked for how *regular and routine* the principals' formal communications were with their faculties. Also, we sought to discover to what extent and with what degree of satisfaction the teachers were participating in *schoolwide decision making.* Our analysis resulted in four administrative styles for communicating with teachers, as shown in Figure 4.1.

*(1) The democratic style.* Principals exhibiting a democratic style of administration provided regular and routine avenues for faculty communication *and* facilitated teachers' collaborative participation in schoolwide decision making. For example, democratic principals held faculty meetings to provide teachers the opportunity to discuss issues important to them about curriculum, instruction, student behavior, and extracurricular activities. Unlike Fred Jensen—Betty Ann Swisher's principal, whose meetings were characterized by his giving information and directions without discussion—democratic principals sought teacher interaction, listened carefully to teachers, and tried to help teachers reach decisions collaboratively.

Some democratic principals also used methods of decision making during faculty meetings, such as taking polls, majority votes, and consensus discussions. Democratic principals of large schools, particularly secondary schools, had created their own version of Likert's link-pin structure (1961), as described in Chapter 2 and again below, by assigning department heads or team leaders the responsibility of communicating up and down between administrators and teachers and across between departments and teams.

Elementary principals more frequently than secondary principals were engaged in democratic administration. Overall, the number of democratic administrators was low, however, compared with the number of those who exhibited nondemocratic administrative styles. Specifically, we classified only 10 of 46 secondary and 15 of 38 elementary principals as democratic.

Of the 10 female elementary principals, 9 were democratic. Indeed, a remarkable result of our study was that women, more often than men, conspicuously initiated and nurtured higher amounts of teacher communication, collegial teamwork, instructional committees, and staff cooperation in reaching decisions. Typically, the women held faculty meetings once a week or twice a month. They had an active committee structure in place and visited most classrooms at least once per week. This finding corroborates the research literature indicating that female administrators more than males engage in collaborative and participatory leadership (see Shakeshaft, 1987).

*(2) The authoritarian style.* Principals exhibiting an authoritarian style provided regular and routine avenues for mostly one-way communication with teachers and did *not* engage the teachers in making schoolwide decisions. Fred Jensen demonstrated the prototype of this style. Although he did call regular meetings, he brought all input to the meetings by controlling the agenda, and he made decisions without formal teacher input. As one principal told us, "I tell them what they need to know. And they do what they need to do."

Indeed, authoritarian principals offered very few opportunities for teacher feedback and discussion. Instead, they communicated with teachers through selected one-on-one conversations, loudspeaker announcements, memos, and unilateral communication at staff meetings. Seldom did the authoritarian principals engage teachers even in informal conversations in the lounge, hallways, or classrooms.

An outspoken kindergarten teacher in Texas spoke about her principal in this way: "What voice do we have? Ha! None. We have a dictatorship in this school. This principal is just like my dad; that's the age they learned this stuff. If you don't like the captain, get on a different ship."

We categorized 28 secondary and 12 elementary principals as autocratic. All of them were males and 38 of the 40 had been coaches of athletic teams. From our interviews and observation, we surmised that most of them conceived of communication and teamwork as unidirectional and hierarchical, as a kind of military teaming, rather than viewing educational teamwork, like the democratic principals did, as transactional and egalitarian. In contrast to this "male perspective" on teamwork was the "female perspective" of 9 of the 10 female principals. The democratic females were more aware of and more skillful in the give-and-take of interpersonal communication, able to discuss feelings without defensiveness, and aware of the power that can be realized from egalitarian teamwork.

*(3) The laissez-faire style.* Principals exhibiting a laissez-faire, or permissive, style neither provided regular and routine staff communication nor tried to stimulate active teacher collaboration in schoolwide decision making. Laissez-faire principals typically left the teachers alone, creating a school organization in which teachers were autonomous, both from the administration and from one another.

We classified eight secondary and eight elementary principals as laissez-faire. The single female principal who was not democratic was laissez-faire; she was not feeling healthy and in her final year of employment before retirement no longer was calling faculty meetings.

For the most part, our interviews with teachers revealed that they were not pleased with laissez-faire principals, although the 16 principals whom we categorized that way were unaware of their teachers' frustration. The teachers had little idea of what was going on in the district and were frustrated with needing to go around the principal to get information. Many teachers with laissez-faire principals reported feeling lonely and without emotional support in the school.

Fourteen laissez-faire principals, however, seemed pleased with how well things were going in their schools. Even a few teachers thought that their principal's permissive style was just fine. These teachers had seized leadership in the school and were making collaborative decisions without the principal. The large majority of teachers, however, were unhappy with their laissez-faire principals. One of them told us, "This year we had only one staff meeting. That was the only time to express any common concerns. Any factory that would do that would be bankrupt. People need to work together!"

*(4) The casual style.* We derived the categories of the first three administrative styles from the classical field experiments on adult leadership in boys' clubs by White and Lippitt (1960). We thought that White and Lippitt's tripartite system for categorizing leadership styles did adequately characterize most of the principals we studied. We decided, however, that a few principals would be more accurately portrayed by the word *casual*. Casual principals did not provide regular and routine procedures for faculty communication but did strive, at least through informal discussion, to have teachers participate in schoolwide decision making.

The casual administrative style occurred solely in elementary schools, and we found it only in three schools. They were among the smallest schools we visited. One of those schools had five teachers, while the two others, isolated in rural settings, had only two teachers each. All three operated mostly informally with the teachers meeting virtually every day to plan and to debrief.

Even when the teachers taught in separated classrooms, walled off from one another, they communicated informally during recesses, lunch, and before and after school. The principals, usually in charge of at least two schools, visited the teachers only once or twice a week. We supposed that those three schools were remnants of turn-of-the-century rural schools in which a few adults supervised teaching. The small size of the school made communication and collaboration easy. The weakness was, however, that new ideas about teaching and learning were not being discussed by the principals and teachers. Perhaps they had succumbed to what Janis (1972) called "groupthink," wherein a group, sheltered from external influence, views its own untested beliefs dogmatically as the truth.

### PORTRAITS OF FIVE PRINCIPALS

Although we were favorably impressed with most of the 25 democratic principals in the sample, we decided to feature five, in particular, who were doing something innovative and exemplary to enhance teaching and learning. We selected Howard Stevens, a middle school principal in Idaho, who helped his staff work together to solve instructional problems by putting into effect a rendition of Likert's link-pin organizational structure. We picked Mary Wright, an Iowa-based elementary principal, because she was unique in making use of a decision-making procedure drawn from research on organization development. We also chose Pam Armstrong, an elementary principal in the heart of Texas, who was building staff acceptance of peer coaching about classroom instruction. Madeline Hunter would have smiled upon her. And we selected Bill Wells, a Montana-based high school principal, for his creative ingenuity in attracting consultants to his isolated school. Finally, we picked Sandy Gregory, an elementary principal in Illinois, who with a team of teachers had created a fair and humane discipline procedure for coping with "undermotivated youngsters."

### *Howard Stevens*

Stevens, at 42, had been the principal of Green Middle School since its inception three years previously. Having recently completed a master's program at a college of education more than 250 miles away, he was enthusiastic about his staff of 40 teachers and committed to applying the concepts and practices of participatory management, which he had learned in graduate school.

Stevens believed wholeheartedly in the democratic style of school administration. He delighted in telling us about how devoted his favorite professor in graduate school was to Douglas McGregor (1967). McGregor wrote that leadership behavior emanates from one's belief about human motivation. If one believes that humans are lazy, are unwilling to improve, and shirk responsibility, leadership will be controlling and dictatorial (Theory X). On the other hand, if one believes that humans are motivated by curiosity, and want to improve and act responsibly, leadership will be more democratic (Theory Y).

The professor was convinced that he, Stevens, would become a Theory Y manager. "In emulation of McGregor's Theory Y," Stevens told us, "I believe that teachers are curious and want to grow; they should be allowed the freedom and given the encouragement to discover new ways of doing things." Stevens thought of Green's teachers as his colleagues and believed, in the spirit of McGregor's Theory Y, that they had as much right as he did to make educational decisions.

Because his staff was rather large for a 6-9 graded school, Stevens created the "Advisory Council," consisting of one teacher at each grade level, to act as a leadership team in coordinating the instructional efforts at Green. To get the Advisory Council started, Stevens brought the entire faculty together several times to discuss the idea and how it might work. Then, each grade-level team, which was constituted of 10 teachers, elevated its own representative to the council, with the agreement that membership in the Advisory Council would rotate annually.

When we toured Green, the Advisory Council had been in place for nearly two years. It was meeting once or twice a month, while the grade-level teams were meeting twice a month on different weeks. Classroom teachers were bringing ideas to the council via their representatives, and the council was communicating its ideas and proposals for change back to the grade-level teams via the representatives. Stevens was employing Likert's idea of a link-pin structure, even though he had not read Likert (1961) so far as we could tell.

Impressively, all 40 teachers and Stevens were linked vertically, and many teachers were also connected horizontally, because the Advisory Council had initiated three committees also made up of one teacher from each grade. Those committees focused on (a) helping students make transitions from one grade to another, (b) facilitating teacher growth and instructional improvement, and (c) creating new procedures for student recognition and building student self-esteem.

The whole staff held a daylong in-service meeting annually in late August to select representatives to that school year's Advisory Council and to create the committee themes and membership for the academic year. Also, with Stevens's encouragement and support, the school staff had been meeting for half days in each of October and February to monitor how committee work, staff communication, and schoolwide decision making were going.

## Mary Wright

Wright was 45 when we met her; she had been the principal of Hillside elementary school for two years. One year prior to our tour of her K-6 staff of 22 teachers, Wright, accompanied by her superintendent, had attended a conference on organization development and staff decision making.

Wright and the superintendent both developed an interest in site-based management at that conference and decided to implement a new decision-making procedure when they returned home. We were strongly affected by Wright and her superintendent because they were the only two school administrators we met along the blue highways who had thought of applying organization-development ideas and techniques in their schools.

They sought to clarify the decision-making role, first that of the administrators in the district and then that of the staff members at each school. The procedure they used was similar to one titled "Decision-Making Roles" developed by Schmuck and Runkel (1988, pp. 292-293). Wright and the superintendent drew a matrix in which the columns represented various jobs or status levels and the rows represented topics about which decisions would have to be made (see Figure 4.2).

For example, in clarifying the decision-making roles in Hillside Elementary, the columns consisted of superintendent, curriculum coordinator, business manager, principal (Mary), the leadership team (made up of grade-level representatives), teachers, classified staff, and students. The rows of the matrix for Hillside consisted of hiring new teachers, ordering text books, determining the discipline code,

| Jobs and Status Levels<br><br>Functions | Superintendent | Curriculum Coordinator | Business Manager | Principal (Mary) | Staff Leadership Team | Teachers | Classified Personnel | Students |
|---|---|---|---|---|---|---|---|---|
| Hiring new teachers | V | C | I | V | P | C | I | I |
| Ordering textbooks | C | V | I | P | P | C | I | I |
| Determining the discipline code | C | C | I | V | P | P | C | C |
| Approving professional travel and in-service events | V | V | C | P | P | C | I | I |
| Parent involvement | V | I | I | P | P | C | I | C |
| Homework policy | C | C | I | V | P | P | I | C |
| Hiring and firing classified | V | I | C | A | C | I | I | I |
| Changing report cards | V | I | C | A | C | C | I | I |

I = informed, C = consulted, P = participate, V = veto power, and
A = authority.

**Figure 4.2.** Agreements About Decision-Making Roles at Hillside
School

approving professional travel and in-service training events, determining the proper forms of parent involvement, policy about homework, hiring and firing classified staff, and changing the report cards.
Wright's superintendent carried out a parallel procedure for clarifying decision making by topic with the business manager, the principals, a representative of the teacher professional association, and the
PTA.

The cells of Wright's matrix for Hillside were filled in with letters
I, C, P, V, or A to signify five alternative kinds of influence. The
letter I signified that the position holders would "have to be *informed*"

of the results of decisions to take appropriate action. C stood for "must be *consulted*"; those with C power were to be consulted early so that their ideas could make a difference in the decision. Thus teachers were being consulted when administrators asked for their input before the decision was made. P stood for "must *participate*"; those with P power must take part in making the decision, and at least a majority vote would be necessary before the decision becomes final. V stood for "*veto power*"; those with V power could reverse or block a decision. Finally, A stood for "*authority* to make decision." Those with A power could make the decision and others would be expected to abide by it. With such a method, all relevant parties understood their roles in making decisions about the school. Obviously, the thrust of site-based management would be to vest in teachers more *consultation* and *participation* in decisions.

## Pam Armstrong

Pam Armstrong, 44 years old and very energetic, had been principal of Grimes Elementary School, grades K-5, for five years when we met her. Although she thought that the relationships between the teachers at Grimes were cordial and polite, she was frustrated by how isolated the teachers were. She told us, "If Grimes were one of those schools where you can enter your class directly from outside, like they have in California, the teachers here probably would never talk to one another." Each of Grimes's 20 teachers taught alone in his or her classroom all day long and every day of the week. Armstrong wanted them to become less isolated from one another and to learn more about what was going on in one another's classes.

In reflecting on how she tried to realize more collegial collaborating at Grimes, Armstrong said, "There was a lot of creative teaching going on, particularly in 7 or 8 classrooms, but only I, as the roving supervisor, knew anything about it. I would mention some of the neat things that the most innovative teachers were doing at faculty meetings, but nothing would ever happen from that. Then, I read an article by Beverly Showers about 'peer coaching' [Showers, 1985]. A light bulb switched on in my head and I decided to try out what Showers was writing about."

Armstrong approached first her most secure and competent teachers; she asked four of them, in particular, to try peer coaching. She had them read the article "The Coaching of Teaching" by Joyce and Showers (1982). She also told them about Hunter's ITIP categories and how they could watch one another performing instructional behaviors that fit into Hunter's categories.

Soon other teachers began to tune in on the "new practice at Grimes" as the original four expressed enthusiasm for Joyce and Showers, Hunter, and peer coaching at faculty meetings. Armstrong didn't try to hide the innovation, nor did she try to force it upon anyone, but the overt interest in peer coaching that she and the four teachers manifested could not go unnoticed by the rest of the staff. Another eight teachers volunteered for peer coaching during the second year, and four more joined in during the third year.

When we toured Grimes, all but 4 teachers of the staff of 20 were paired off in "coaching dyads." Not only were the teachers learning about ITIP, but they also were learning about alternative teaching methods by observing one another as well as exploring new ways of cooperating with one another on curriculum development.

## Bill Wells

Wells had grown up in a small, Eastern Montana town and had always planned to return to a small town as a teacher. Upon graduating from teachers' college, however, he decided to "go for the excitement and money" of Minneapolis. He lasted only two years in the city as high school social studies teacher and then returned to the high Montana plains to teach social studies in a small-town high school. Twelve years later, at the young age of 37, he had become the principal of that same high school. We met him two years after that.

When we met Wells in spring 1989, his town was celebrating its centennial. His school, Anderson Senior High, was planning not only for the centennial celebration but also for its third summer institute. Wells and his fellow principals (all of whom were males) had brought an emphasis on staff development to their isolated district. Indeed, Wells was rare among the high school principals we met in his sincere interest in teacher growth and staff development.

By scrimping on pay for substitute teachers and by virtue of a small grant from the state department of education (Wells had written the successful proposal), Wells was bringing in resource people from the county office of education and the University of Montana to run a week-long summer institute for teachers. The Anderson teachers were attending the summer institutes free and also were gaining credits on the district's salary schedule.

Wells had engaged Anderson teachers in deciding upon the topics for the 1989 institute. They were interested to learn more about cooperative learning and portfolio assessment of writing, both very rare interests for senior high teachers in our experience on the blue highways. A few of the teachers, who were earning their master's degrees, were able to obtain university credit. One teacher we interviewed praised the summer institutes as "a great way to bring new ideas to our district." Another summed up her colleagues' sentiments when she told us, "Here we are in the boondocks and feel like we know the cutting edge issues in education." Wells, himself, was conspicuously present at each summer institute, full time and right along with the teachers.

## Sandy Gregory

Gregory, in her early forties and already in a second principalship, was not only upwardly mobile but also ambitious. The principal of a K-6 school in Western Illinois, she told us, "I want people to recognize me as good."

When we met her, Sandy was administering a school in which many families were poor, broken, and living with emotional tension. The growing number of students who needed emotional buttressing could not be handled by the school staff alone. The teachers needed to enlist parent cooperation.

Gregory told us, "One of my jobs here at Baker Elementary is to strengthen the family. It's frightening to me. Maybe we can help train kids to be more resourceful, but we do need some help at home. We work with the kids and parents through discipline; discipline should always be tied to counseling. Through discipline and counseling we hope to motivate the undermotivated, and that goes for both kids and parents."

Gregory and a committee of five teachers had created what they called the "Discipline Assignment Sheet." Its format was designed to instruct and counsel both student and parents about proper academic behavior. After a student had behaved inappropriately three times, he or she was given a copy of the Discipline Assignment Sheet to take home. There the student was obliged to complete the form in collaboration with a parent. The Discipline Assignment Sheet had seven items:

1. What rule(s) did you break at school?
2. What caused you to break that rule?
3. Why do you think the school has the rules(s)?
4. What would it be like at school if lots of students broke the rule(s)?
5. What alternative ways could you have solved your problem?
6. Look up the following words in a dictionary, and write down at least one meaning for each: *responsible, self-control,* and *improve.*
7. List three ways you can improve your self-control and be more responsible at school.

Gregory and her five committee members, all of whom we interviewed, told us that they felt very good about the impact of their Discipline Assignment Sheets. Not only had student motivation toward academic learning improved, but also many more parents than usual were showing interest in the school.

Also, we learned that some items on the assignment sheet were being used by 12 other teachers at Baker to guide discussions with their students about rules, discipline, and appropriate academic behavior. Gregory told us, "The procedure has had the dual advantage of getting our staff to be more consistent about discipline and of getting our parents to act more supportively toward the staff and the academic program at Baker."

## TARGETS OF CHANGE

We asked the principals about their professional reading habits. Most confessed to reading very little educational literature regularly because of too little free time to concentrate on serious reading during the day and too little energy for professional thinking at the end of the day. Most did, however, regularly browse a few professional magazines, the most frequent of which were the Association of Supervision and Curriculum Development's *Educational Leadership* and Phi Delta Kappa's *The Kappan*.

After returning to Oregon, we did an analysis of article titles in those two magazines for the numbers issued in 1988 and the first half of 1989, the months just preceding and during our time on tour. The most frequent topics with direct relevance for school administration were fostering staff collegiality and collaboration, dealing with multiculturalism and diversity, facilitating site-based management, and moving from a focus on school management toward a focus on instructional leadership. In short, the most frequent topics in *Educational Leadership* and *The Kappan* during 1988 and 1989 dealt with improving academic instruction by using workplace democracy in the school.

Our interviews and observations, however, showed that most administrators and teachers had little knowledge or even concern with what the professional literature could tell them about the benefits of democratic participation in schools. Among the 123 administrators we met (84 principals, 25 superintendents, and 14 district office personnel), only 2, Mary Wright and her superintendent, were using ideas and techniques drawn from the field of *organization development.* Out of 119 teachers, only 10 recognized the term *cooperative learning;* 5 of them were Judy Landry's colleagues. Only 20 teachers acknowledged deliberately trying to teach their students social skills by using classroom learning groups. In only eight elementary schools, one middle school, and one senior high did we find teachers actively and regularly engaged with the principals in problem solving and decision making.

The absence of genuine staff collaboration and classroom cooperation in small districts might be understood better by considering the load carried by administrators and teachers. We saw superintendents, for example, not only wrestling with budgets, working on curriculum, and meeting with board members but also driving buses, attending out-of-town sports events, and directing traffic. We saw principals not only supervising teachers, running staff meetings, and observing classes and hall behavior but also acting as athletic directors, working on bus schedules, and coordinating the curriculum for the district. We even saw one district in Texas in which the principals worked without school secretaries. We saw teachers teaching up to seven hours a day without time for preparation or grading papers, and then spending two or three hours supervising extracurricular activities after school. Perhaps educators of small districts are unskillful at collaboration because they are overworked and stuck in routines and rituals that keep them from cooperating.

In *The Collaborative School,* Smith and Scott (1990) presented research and experiential evidence from educators to show that staff collaboration is key to effective instruction. In particular, such practices as mutual help, exchange of ideas, joint planning, peer coaching, and teacher participation in schoolwide decision making have been affirmed by research on both effective schools and productive workplaces in business and industry.

The single, most persuasive research endeavor on staff collaboration was carried out by Rosenholtz (1989). She gathered data from 78 elementary schools in eight Tennessee-based school districts and showed various benefits of staff collaboration, including enhanced teacher performance and student learning. Indeed, staff collaboration was a predictor of student achievement gains in reading and math. Rosenholtz measured the achievement patterns of a single cohort of students as they moved from second to fifth grade. Her statistical analysis, showing achievement gains in collaborative schools, corroborated some previously persuasive case studies on the benefits of staff collaboration by Rutter et al. (1979), Little (1982), Purkey and Smith (1983), and Bacharach et al. (1984). By the time of our tour in 1989, the professional literature clearly had more than a couple of articles on the benefits of the collaborative school.

In our text, *Group Processes in the Classroom* (in its 6th edition in 1992), we drew on research in social psychology conducted during the 1970s and the 1980s to show that a collaborative school climate can set the stage not only for student growth in academic achievement but also for student cooperation and mutual helpfulness in the classroom. Research demonstrated, for example, that teachers who practice communication and meeting skills with one another in their adult, professional exchanges also tend to use similar communication skills with their students in the classroom. Also, teachers who are comfortable cooperating with one another tend to feel comfortable asking their students to cooperate in the classroom. The teachers of a collaborative school view the school as a community of humans engaged in I-Thou relationships, cooperative learning, and cooperative development. They believe that power should be shared by all, including the students, and that, whenever feasible, decisions should be made by those who will be affected by the decisions.

The starting point for development of the collaborative school rests in the role of the principal. In particular, principals must build into their roles the concepts and skills of participative management and instructional leadership. They should begin to emulate the best of Howard Stevens, Mary Wright, Pam Armstrong, Bill Wells, and Sandy Gregory. Here are a few specific targets for change.

## *Fostering Effective Meetings*

Buber (1958) taught that life is a series of meetings or interpersonal exchanges, and that life takes on special meaning and significance for individuals through their I-Thou exchanges. The staff meetings that we observed were seldom meaningful to the teachers and hardly ever consisted of I-Thou exchanges. We believe that improving the meaningfulness of staff meetings should be a primary target for principals.

Principals of small districts should recognize the potential benefits of formal meetings with committees, departments, teams, and faculties

for organizing curricula, developing policy, and upgrading instruction. One of the greatest values of effective meetings is that they
draw out and coordinate staff members' ideas for a systematic
exchange of creative solutions to instructional problems. It was
through meetings with small groups of teachers that Mary Wright
clarified decision-making roles at Hillside and Sandy Gregory created the Discipline Assignment Sheet at Baker. But, even the sim-
plest matters, such as using the library, audiovisual equipment, the
copy machine, or art supplies, can be difficult for faculty members
to coordinate and might be facilitated by staff discussions.

Groups of teachers, when the individuals are truly collaborating,
can produce more ideas, stimulate more creative thought among
members, pool ideas to build more realistic forecasts of the consequences of decisions, and produce bolder plans than can individual
teachers working alone. The most important asset of a good meeting
is that teachers and administrators can commit themselves to acting
on a group agreement in one another's presence.

Effective meetings consist of sticking to an agenda while checking
individuals' understandings and involvement, maintaining focus on task
in the group while encouraging participants to be open about their personal views, dispersing leadership functions and responsibilities while
keeping a clear understanding of who is chairing the process, and ending
with a clear understanding of the decisions made and the expected actions
to be taken between meetings. Five procedures should be kept in mind by
the principal trying to make staff meetings more effective:

*(1) Preparing an agenda.* Because most school meetings consist of
several topics or activities that vary in their content and respective
time requirements, it is important to have an agenda clearly printed
on a chalkboard, poster paper, or an overhead projector. Some
agenda items will be presented for information only; others will
require longer discussion, decision making, and planning for action.
The principal can help a staff improve efficiency by spending a brief
time at the beginning of the meeting to set priorities in the agenda,
designate approximate time allotments, and decide what kind of
action each item will require. Figure 4.3 presents an illustration of
an agenda used by an elementary staff in Oregon.

| Agenda Item | Order | Time | Person | Required Action |
|---|---|---|---|---|
| School climate | 1 | 15 | Dave | Discuss, appoint subcommittee |
| Open house | 2 | 5 | Principal | Information only |
| New math textbook | 3 | 20 | Curriculum Committee | Decision |
| Playground rules | 4 | 10 | Joan | Advise aides |
| Debriefing | 5 | 5 | All | Discuss |

**Figure 4.3.** Illustrative Agenda Format of an Elementary Staff

In the column titled "Person" are listed the names of the people who will lead the discussion of that agenda item. Dave, the current chair of the School Climate Committee, presented ideas from the committee about how to improve school climate and asked for advice on how to appoint a subcommittee to take action. After the principal informed the staff about a few details on the forthcoming school open house, the Curriculum Committee, consisting of seven teachers, divided the staff into seven equal-sized small groups for discussion about a new math text. The whole staff came to a decision by voting after the small group discussions. Joan, chair of the "Nuts and Bolts" Committee, told the staff about a few new rules and said that she and the vice-principal would be advising the aides about the new rules. The debriefing consisted of praising the Curriculum Committee for its conscientious work on the new math text.

*(2) Convening the meeting.* Every meeting we observed was chaired by the official superordinate of the group: Board meetings were led by the board president; district administrator meetings were chaired by the superintendent; school meetings were chaired by the principal. Similar to our classroom observations, the chairs, particularly the principals with teachers, dominated the time during the meetings. More than half of the faculty meetings we observed were similar to the one chaired by Fred Jensen in Betty Ann Swisher's school in North Dakota. Board meetings and those convened by superintendents

were typically more participatory compared with school faculty meetings.

It is very important to have one person convening a meeting, but that person does not have to be the official superordinate of the group. In fact, staff meetings in schools can go much better when the role of convener rotates through the staff. In other words, over a series of meetings, each staff member takes on the role of convener.

Conveners act as facilitators. They facilitate discussion by keeping the group on task, calling on silent people, asking brief questions, and summarizing concisely. Before the meeting, the convener reviews the agenda and sets up the room. During the meeting, the convener keeps the group on task, is attuned to confusion, tries to clarify, checks to make sure that everyone has a chance to speak, and summarizes or asks someone else to summarize the decisions that have been made. Finally, the convener conducts a debriefing discussion during the last part of the meeting.

*(3) Recording the outcomes.* We observed a number of faculty meetings in which no official record whatsoever was kept about the outcomes of the meeting. And, in most of those meetings in which a record was kept, it was the school secretary who kept the minutes. Meetings can be run more efficiently and lead to better follow-through after they are over when one regular member of the staff has the role of recorder. The recorder does more than just write down the decisions of the group. The recorder helps the convener to keep the group on task and to summarize orally the decisions of the group. The recorder records the major views expressed under each agenda item and, at the end of each agenda item, records a brief summary, containing decisions made, understandings achieved, and action to be taken.

After the meeting, the recorder and convener should check the clarity and completeness of the record. They should also make sure that agenda items not completed are put on the agenda of the next meeting. Effective groups assign recording tasks to one individual but also rotate the role throughout the membership just as the convener role is rotated.

*(4) Using communication skills.* The principal can single-handedly facilitate more I-Thou exchanges at faculty meetings by using good

communication skills. First, keep in mind that communication consists of *both* sending and receiving a message. We observed all too frequently, in faculty meetings of small districts, that the intention of the principal rarely matched the impact on the teachers, and that the teachers' underlying frustrations with the principal's style were not coming across to the principal. The communication skills of paraphrasing, summarizing, and impression checking should be used more, particularly by the principal as a role model for the teachers.

Second, keep in mind that there are at least two levels of meaning in every message: the content and the interpersonal relationship. Teachers are sensitive, particularly to the interpersonal relationship they have with their principal. Principals must remember to communicate one-on-one often with every teacher in the school. And, in these one-on-one exchanges, it is important for the principal to describe his or her own feelings, to listen carefully to the feelings of the teacher, and to encourage the teacher to strive to satisfy his or her own feelings and values in the school.

Third, keep in mind that silence does *not* indicate agreement and that frequently silence is a common response to school system conflict, particularly when the conflict is between the administration and the teachers. Principals need to watch how teachers respond physically to their statements at meetings and to cultivate the skill of impression checking. Impression checking consists of describing what you perceive to be the other person's emotional state to determine whether you have accurately decoded his or her expressions of feelings. Skillful impression checking requires the principal to read nonverbal cues, to draw tentative inferences from them, to describe clearly the inferred feeling, and to indicate the inferential character of the impression.

Finally, keep in mind that positive reinforcement is often infrequent and ineffectively applied on school staffs. Principals must remember to praise their teachers often, both in public gatherings and one-on-one. Moreover, they should remember to spread the praise more or less equally throughout the staff. Direct, positive reinforcement generates personal satisfaction among teachers and is perhaps more needed nowadays than ever before because of the widespread public criticism of the teaching profession.

*(5) Debriefing meeting processes.* The principal should demonstrate an interest in school improvement by advocating self-assessment and self-renewal. One concrete way to do that is by encouraging process debriefings as part of the meeting agenda. The convener can, for example, conduct a debriefing discussion during the last few minutes of the meeting by asking staff members to consider the following: Did we accomplish our goals for this meeting? Are there agenda items that we will need to return to in the future? Are we getting everyone to participate and contribute? Did we avoid pitfalls such as wasting time? What sorts of things did I, the convener, do to help the group move through the agenda? Are there some other things we'd like to see future conveners do? What about things the recorder did to help us? Are there things we'd like future recorders to do?

Another activity related to improving meetings is the collection of formal questionnaire data about them. Some school staffs with which we have consulted in California, Oregon, and Washington have used the "Meetings Questionnaire" developed by Matthew Miles and published in Schmuck and Runkel (1988, pp. 159-161). The principal can ask each staff member who meets with him or her regularly to respond to the 37 items on the questionnaire. The principal can then tabulate and display these data on poster paper to present means and frequency distributions for each item. Teachers can be encouraged to diagnose their own meetings by discussing items on which high agreement exists or those items with mixed responses. A six-point scale, ranging from high typicality to low typicality, is used for each item. A few item examples follow: "When problems come up in the meeting, they are thoroughly explored until everyone understands what the problem is." "Someone summarizes progress from time to time." Additional questionnaires for assessing the quality of staff meetings can be found in Jorde-Bloom, Sherer, and Britz (1991).

## *Establish Link-Pin Structures*

Rensis Likert (1961) first pointed out that the real guts or lifeblood of any organization are its face-to-face groups, consisting of supervisors and the subordinates who are immediately responsible to them. He went on to argue that the face-to-face groups should be linked upward in the organization, so that the groups lower in the hierarchy have the capability of communicating with and thereby influencing higher levels of the organization. In Likert's link-pin organizational structure, supervisors are members of at least two face-to-face groups: the group for which they have leadership responsibility and the group to which they are responsible. Howard Stevens was the only principal we met on our tour who was self-consciously using the link-pin structure at Green Middle School.

But Stevens had taken a step beyond Likert in also linking teachers horizontally within Green Middle School. He did that by establishing committees consisting of at least one teacher from each grade-level team. In the parlance of organizational development, Stevens was creating a "matrix organization." The matrix organization has face-to-face work groups linked vertically and horizontally. Thus, in schools, grade-level teams or subject matter departments are linked to principals through the participation of team leaders or department heads, both in a leadership cabinet and in their team or department, *and* grade-level teams or subject matter departments are linked to one another through the participation of teachers in committees or task forces made up of representatives from each team or department.

We have been consulting at Benton Elementary School, in a suburb of Portland, Oregon, which has developed a wonderful example of a matrix organization. A larger K-6 school, Benton has a professional faculty of 44 teachers and specialists. The principal, an assistant principal, and eight faculty members constitute "the Benton Leadership Team." The eight faculty members come one each from kindergarten, grades 1-6, and the specialists. Benton also has four schoolwide committees, each made up of from 9 to 12 members with representatives from each grade level and the specialists. The committees are as follows. The School Climate Committee is to boost school pride and spirit by developing and implementing programs focused on positive reinforcement of student accomplishments, student self-esteem, and a unique Benton identity. The Care Team is to generate programs to increase feelings of success for students with special needs, to act as a clearinghouse for ideas about how best to serve "at-risk" students, and to give support to colleagues who are facing the challenge of working closely with troubled students. The Curriculum and Instruction Task Force is to select, organize, and present new curriculum goals and materials to the staff and to give support to teachers who are trying new curricula or instructional techniques. Finally, the Schoolwide Procedures Committee is to keep Benton running smoothly by dealing with concerns about school procedures such as discipline cases, fire drills, scheduling, and school rules.

## Facilitating Faculty Collaboration

In her dissertation, *The Principal as an Agent of Change* (1984), Barbara Keirnes-Young did a content analysis of more than 150 articles and books on the role of the principal that had been published before 1984. In particular, she searched for what the professional literature had said about principals acting effectively as agents of instructional improvement. She came up with four roles that effective principals perform:

1. The *action researcher* sees that evaluative data are collected regularly and then uses the data to facilitate instructional improvement.
2. The *social architect* seeks to build cooperation and collaboration among teachers and uses such entities as teams, cabinets, committees, task forces, quality circles, link-pin structures, and informal groups to do so.
3. The *staff developer* seek ways to help and support teachers' growth in instructional skill. The staff developer is concerned simultaneously with personal, professional growth and with organizational development of the school.
4. The *political strategist* seeks to build coalitions within the school and with key people outside the school to achieve better student learning. The political strategist deals directly and effectively with conflict.

For the principals of small-district schools to move toward instructional leadership, they will have to take on more of the characteristics of action researchers, social architects, staff developers, and political strategists.

In striving to be action researchers, the principals can take initiative to model their openness and willingness to change themselves by soliciting feedback about themselves and by demonstrating new actions that are based on the feedback. For example, the principal might ask teachers to respond anonymously to three questions: (a) What are some things I should do more often to make your teaching effective? (b) What are some things I should be doing less often to make your teaching effective? (c) What are some things I should keep doing as I am right now? After those data have been analyzed, the principal should pick some aspect of his or her role behavior to change and let all teachers in the school know that change is being tried. As action researcher, the principal also could encourage the use of a climate questionnaire to uncover any problems of staff or student morale that might exist in the school. After those data have been analyzed, the principal should facilitate responses to the problems by encouraging and supporting teachers to try some new activities. We found no principal on the blue highways who was doing action research.

As social architect, the principal articulates school tasks that need to be worked on, goes to individual teachers or clusters of teachers to enlist their interest in the tasks, listens to the teachers' concerns about the tasks, and initiates formal faculty subgroups to work on the tasks. The principal as social architect should be concerned with putting the right people together to work on a task. During the time as social architect, the principal is concerned with running efficient and effective meetings, as we wrote about above.

In striving to take leadership in staff development, the principal needs to demonstrate his or her own desire to develop new skills, either by attending in-service training workshops for teachers with the teachers, as Bill Wells did when professors from the University of Montana brought a summer institute to his district, or by attending training sessions especially for school leaders, as Mary Wright and her superintendent did when they attended a conference on organization development and staff decision making in Iowa. The principal as staff developer also persuades faculty members of their need for personal development, refresher courses, renewal, and the like. In other words, the principal goes directly to individual staff members, frequently informally, to encourage them to develop themselves further.

One successful vehicle for stimulating professional development is for the principal to appoint a staff development committee in the school, which would have the task of diagnosing teachers' needs for development and arranging programs of in-service education. Bill Wells had established a teacher committee to do just that prior to the third summer institute in his district. He had set aside regular time in faculty meetings for that committee to interview teachers about their needs and to present their plans for the 1989 summer institute.

As political strategist, the principal initiates strategic and tactical communications with power centers, both within and outside the school. The principal watches for informal coalitions on the staff and seeks to work with them on behalf of everyone's goals. The principal also maintains regular communication with key role takers in the superintendent's office. As political strategist, the principal also strives to manage efficient and effective public relations, understanding that the students and teachers in small districts are active communicators in the community and therefore that they are important public relations agents. Maintaining satisfied students and teachers will go a long way toward keeping the community satisfied with the school.

Many of the 25 principals we categorized as democratic were clearly good at social architecture and political strategy. Fewer were acting effectively as leaders of staff development, and no one was actively pursuing action research. A turnaround of instruction in the schools of small districts could begin if the principals would start to act more vigorously than they do now as instructional leaders.

## REFERENCES

Bacharach, S. B., et al. (1984). *Paying for better teaching: Merit pay and its alternatives.* Ithaca, NY: Organizational Analysis and Practice, Inc.

Buber, M. (1958). *I and thou.* New York: Scribner.

Janis, I. (1972). *Victims of groupthink.* Boston: Houghton Mifflin.

Jorde-Bloom, P., Sherer, M., & Britz, J. (1991). *Blueprint for action: Achieving center-based change through staff development.* Lake Forest, IL: New Horizons (distributed by Gryphon House).

Joyce, B., & Showers, B. (1982). The coaching of teaching. *Educational Leadership, 40*(1), 4-8.

Keirnes-Young, B. (1984). *The principal as an agent of change.* Unpublished doctoral dissertation, University of Oregon.

Least Heat Moon, W. (1982). *The blue highways: A journey into America.* New York: Fawcett Crest.

Likert, R. (1961). *New patterns of management.* New York: McGraw-Hill.

Little, J. W. (1982). Norms of collegiality and experimentation: Workplace conditions of school success. *American Educational Research Journal, 19*(3), 325-340.

Mayer, M. (1961). *The schools.* New York: Harper.

McGregor, D. (1967). *The professional manager.* New York: McGraw-Hill.

Purkey, S., & Smith, M. (1983, March). Effective schools: A review. *The Elementary School Journal,* pp. 427-452.

Rosenholtz, S. (1989). *Teacher workplace: The social organization of schools.* New York: Longman.

Rutter, M., et al. (1979). *Fifteen thousand hours: Secondary schools and their effects on children.* Cambridge, MA: Harvard University Press.

Schmuck, R., & Runkel, P. (1988). *Handbook of organization development in schools* (3rd ed.). Prospect Heights, IL: Waveland.

Schmuck, R., & Schmuck, P. (1992). *Group processes in the classroom* (6th ed.). Dubuque, IA: William C Brown.

Shakeshaft, C. (1987). *Women in educational administration.* Beverly Hills, CA: Sage.

Showers, B. (1985). Teachers coaching teachers. *Educational Leadership, 42*(7), 43-48.

Smith, S., & Scott, J. (1990). *The collaborative school: A work environment for effective instruction.* Eugene: University of Oregon, ERIC Clearinghouse on Educational Management.

White, R., & Lippitt, R. (1960). *Autocracy and democracy.* New York: Harper.

# 5

△
▢

# Superintendents

## BECOMING COMMUNITY LEADERS

He who trims himself to suit everybody will soon whittle himself away.

Education does not have the answer alone, but without education there is no answer.

When I feel true wisdom, I'll let you know, if letting you know is still important.

The greatest problem in communication is the illusion that it has been achieved.

Tell me, I forget
Show me, I remember
Involve me, I understand

A society is judged by how well it treats its children.

*—Signs in superintendents' offices*

On hearing us enumerate the obscure names of districts we would visit, a cosmopolitan teacher friend, who frequently attends London theater during Christmas breaks, responded, "Those are just the sorts of places I carefully avoid." A part of us agreed with him, but we did, after all, deliberately choose to drive the two-lane secondary roads and to eschew districts near colleges of education. It was therefore incidental when we passed through university towns. Still, we grew to anticipate them like a Pavlovian dog anticipates the smell of ground beef.

We collect university towns much as other people collect antiques, baseball cards, and compact discs. We search for them and file them away in our minds. We'd rather walk about in Ann Arbor, Lawrence, or Norman than other towns in Michigan, Kansas, and Oklahoma. Our favorites on this trip were Las Cruces, New Mexico; Grambling, Louisiana; Oxford, Mississippi; Macomb, Illinois; Grand Forks, North Dakota; and Missoula, Montana. We confess even to traveling a little out of the way to spend weekends in three of them. All we wanted on tour we could find in those towns: national public radio, a restaurant that did more than fry food, and a bookstore or two with more than religious titles.

Indeed, a bookstore became our sought-after Shangri-la, because reading was our primary form of entertainment, and the White Tortoise simply was not large enough to store a library. Reading, too, offered welcome relief from the arduous rigor of interviewing, observing, and recording our data. We never watched television. We never went to the concert hall, the opera house, or the legitimate stage, and we infrequently saw a movie, although we shall never forget watching *Mississippi Burning* in a racially integrated cinema in Jackson, Mississippi. Like Gary Ritter, we have "a fundamental belief in reading," and we will read just about anything.

From the very beginning of our tour, we decided to focus on authors who had lived in or written about the regions of our itinerary: John Steinbeck in California; Frank Dobie and Larry McMurtry in Texas; William Faulkner and Eudora Welty in Mississippi; Ellen Gilcrist in Arkansas; Mark Twain in Missouri; Carl Sandburg in Illinois; Ernest Hemingway in Upper Michigan; F. Scott Fitzgerald in Minnesota; Ivan Doig in Montana; and Barry Lopez and Ken Kesey in Oregon.

We also took along a few classics on American culture that we had read before. On tour, we reread Alex de Tocqueville's *Democracy in America,* Bellah et al.'s *Habits of the Heart,* Reisman's *The Lonely Crowd,* The Lynds' *Middletown,* Warner's *Social Class in America,* Silberman's *Crisis in the Classroom,* and Mayer's *The Schools.* To focus on small-district schools, we reread Barker and Gump's *Big School, Small School,* Fuller's *The Old Country School,* McLaren's *Life in Schools,* and Peshkin's *Growing Up American,* and we took along a few travel books, such as Steinbeck's *Travels With Charlie* and Theroux's *Patagonia Express.* Of course, Least Heat Moon's *The Blue Highways* always was by our side.

Lest we give the impression, however, of haughtiness about our choice of reading matter, we hasten to add that our preferred genre for relaxation was the mystery novel. Our favorite authors were Amanda Cross, Dick Francis, P. D. James, Ruth Rendell, Josephine Tey, Margaret Truman, and M. K. Wren. We came to appreciate used bookstores that traded books with customers. We found the best selections of paperback mysteries stashed in two-for-one shops in Cape Girardeau, Missouri; Wisconsin Rapids, Wisconsin; and, the most delightful of all, in Grand Forks, North Dakota.

As we read, we often listened to classical music on a small cassette recorder. At times, the sounds were so powerful in the confined space of the Tortoise that we would lose our concentration and look up from our books. One recording that stirred us, time and time again, was that of Ravel's orchestral transcription of *Pictures From an Exhibition,* originally written by Mussorgsky for piano.

Ravel uses a solo trumpet at the beginning of *Pictures* to attract the listener's attention with its clarion announcement of a theme that reappears throughout the work. Each new painting is, in turn, introduced briefly by the rich and mellow tones of a trumpet, followed by other brass, woodwinds, strings, and percussion, until, at the end, in an awesome and convulsive climax, reminiscent of the finish of Ravel's *Bolero,* every instrument joins in unison to play the theme originally stated by the solo trumpet. The trumpet no longer can be heard; every instrument is gradually combined and blended into an elegant crescendo. We decided that the superintendent should play first trumpet for the small district.

### THE SUPERINTENDENTS WE STUDIED

We interviewed 25 superintendents each for more than two hours, shadowed them for parts of three consecutive days and evenings, and observed them in formal meetings with the board or their principals. We also interviewed 84 principals, 119 teachers, and 28 board members, in part, about their superintendents.

Because the scholarly monographs of Gross, Mason, and McEachern (1958), Carlson (1970), Cuban (1976, 1988), Wissler and Ortiz (1988), and Blumberg (1985) highlighted urban and suburban superintendents, we sought to study whether the superintendents of small districts would see their role differently. For example, we wondered if superintendents in small districts would invite more participation and collaboration from their administrators and teachers than their big-district counterparts. Would they take an active role in curriculum and instructional leadership? Would they act as community leaders? We sought to describe their personal characteristics, to find out what their days were like, to take stock of their beliefs, and to describe any exemplary practices, that we could find, in participatory management and instructional leadership.

The prototypical superintendent was a white male in his early fifties, with coaching experience, working in the same geographic region where he grew up, with nearly 30 years' experience in professional education, more than 8 years of which were spent as a superintendent in his current district. In fact, all 25 were white men, 2 of whom were Hispanic. Their mean age was 52 with a bell-shaped distribution ranging from 42 to 66. Only three had earned doctorates. Thirteen had been coaches of athletic teams.

In the course of interviewing Jamie Stowell, a superintendent in Mississippi, he pointed out of his office window to a couple of nearby houses and said, "My Granddaddy lived there, my Dad lived there, and I live right there." Of the 25, 21 superintendents had been born in the same state in which they were currently working, and most of them were working less than 100 miles from where they grew up. The four superintendents who were from out of state had chosen to move west to get away from crowded conditions. The mean years of tenure in their current position was 8.6, but the distribution ranged from 2 to 24. Eighteen superintendents definitely were not planning to move, while ten were actively planning to retire nearby. Our sample of small-district superintendents was decidedly *local.*

## LIVES OF SUPERINTENDENTS IN SMALL DISTRICTS

We learned that superintendents of small districts have to be adept at all trades. Like their suburban and urban counterparts, they work with board policies, budgets, curricula, facilities, laws, and personnel, but they do much, much more than that. For example, we saw them:

- accompanying board members on a tour of a steel mill;
- attending Kiwanis, Lions, and Rotary meetings;
- coaching the girls' junior high basketball team;
- directing traffic as school was letting out;
- driving a bus load of students out of town;
- eating pancakes and sausage at a church supper;
- meeting with a regional, special education consortium;
- performing in a high school musical; and
- picking up district mail at the post office.

They were engaged in district work often from 7 a.m. till almost midnight. We saw them at both ends of the day, from eating breakfast with hungry elementary students to bringing home tired secondary students from a basketball tournament after a one-way bus ride of 175 miles.

Because many of the small-district superintendents had only a secretary and an uncertificated business manager, they were, themselves, *the district,* picking up everything from mail to a team without a coach. One superintendent in Texas talked sardonically about the job: "Superintendents of small school districts are a ridiculous catchall," he said, "mostly doing things that have little to do with classroom instruction. Fill pop machines, refill coffee pots, put up the flag, take down the flag, clean up asbestos, check for lead in the water, fix the furnace, and now test for radon. All that's enough to drive you crazy. I've already received three advertisements about checking for radon. That's what drives me nuts. It's a year unusually full of baloney."

We were not surprised, after hearing statements like that, to find out that most of our interviewees had very little time to read. Although 15 received *The American School Board Journal* and *The Executive Educator* at their offices, 11 confessed that they barely had enough time to skim them. Two others mentioned a preference for *Education Digest,* because they could read it quickly. Three others, who had recently been senior high principals, continued to receive the *Bulletin of the National Association of Secondary School Principals,* but they too had little time to read the articles.

As we probed them about why they didn't read more, a superintendent in Wisconsin admitted, "I don't read; I play golf." Indeed, golf was a favorite pastime for 14 of the 25. A superintendent in Arizona sheepishly confessed, "It takes me six months to read an article or a book, and by then I'm tired of it." A superintendent in Iowa told us, "I depend on my principals for reading material, especially the two who are working on their superintendent's credential." In short, the superintendents we met on the tour did not, by and large, assume leadership with regard to the professional literature.

Nor did many of the superintendents read much for relaxation or escape. A few said they admired Robert Ludlum's spy novels and James Michener's historical fiction. Larry McMurtry's *Lonesome Dove* was being read by two Texas-based superintendents, at the time during the winter of 1989 when it was being enacted on television, but Louis L'Amour's Westerns won hands down as the favorites of 10 of the superintendents. An embarrassed superintendent in Illinois told us that he had recently finished rereading Shakespeare's *Romeo and Juliet* but then defensively added, "My wife is an English teacher, you see, and she got me into it."

Popular magazines read by the superintendents were *Field and Stream, Sports Illustrated, Reader's Digest,* and *Progressive Farmer.*

Most of them felt satisfied, however, if they could just get through the local newspaper. Our results reminded us of a Chinese proverb we had seen printed on a poster in the library of an elementary school in Washington: *A Book Is Like a Garden Carried in the Pocket.* By the time we returned to Oregon, we felt discouraged that more of the superintendents we met weren't carrying flower seeds in their pockets.

But, after all, when you are on the "public stage" for most waking hours, how can you find time to read? One superintendent put it this way, "The school is where everything happens in this community, and the people expect me to be visible. They have a deep interest in their children, and expect me to show an even deeper interest. I feel that I always should be available to the parents, the students, and my fellow educators." Another superintendent told us, "In this town, school activities become bigger than life." Except for some long-term senior high principals, the small-district superintendents, also, were "bigger than life." They were the most visible and important public figures in their towns.

## SUPERINTENDENTS' MANAGEMENT STYLES

As we did with the principals, we sought to characterize the superintendents' management styles. This time our categories were slightly different.

We categorized 11 superintendents as *collaborative.* Our observations and interviews showed that those 11 worked comfortably in groups, fostered equality among themselves and their colleagues, and conscientiously sought input and shared influence. Second, we categorized another 11 superintendents as *one-on-one.* They tended to avoid group meetings in favor of meetings with individuals in their office, to foster a social hierarchy in which they were clearly the boss, and to seek dominating influence in their interpersonal exchanges.

The two initial categories for superintendents were similar to the democratic and authoritarian categories for the principals, except that the authoritarianism of the superintendents was more subtle than that of the principals. The authoritarian superintendents tended to disguise their dominating supervision by meeting one-on-one frequently with their principals and teacher leaders.

The third category was *laissez-faire* in which we placed the other three superintendents. They avoided group meetings almost entirely, fostered a lonely autonomy among their principals, and sought always to delegate or to avoid duties.

It is important to note that whether superintendents were collaborative, one-on-one, or laissez-faire was unrelated to age, geographic region, and amount of graduate education. Also, the three management styles of superintendents did not seem to be associated with the reading habits of the superintendents we interviewed. They did differ, however, in the accomplishments about which they were proud, the challenges that they faced, and their views about gender equity.

## ACCOMPLISHMENTS OF THE SUPERINTENDENTS

We asked each superintendent to reflect on accomplishments in his current position. They most often talked about four accomplishments:

### Accomplishment 1: Erecting or Remodeling Facilities

- "We just built a wonderful middle school and it was named after me" (Texas).
- "Isn't this a beautiful gymnasium? It will bring more basketball tournaments to our district" (North Dakota).
- "We built this great wing on our still-expanding elementary school last year. I'm proud of the community support I was able to muster for this construction" (Texas).

### Accomplishment 2: Fiscal Saving and Scrimping

- "We were able to build a new school from budgetary savings rather than a bond issue" (Wisconsin).

- "We've invested the district funds at high rates of interest and I'm proud of that" (New Mexico).
- "I've eliminated the secretaries from our elementary schools and that has helped us meet our bills" (Texas).

## Accomplishment 3: Initiating Curriculum Development

- "I'm proud of our teachers' committees to work on changes in the scope and sequence of our elementary curriculum and the instructional strategies at our middle school" (California).
- "I like how we've been successful in attracting curriculum consultants to our district from the state department" (Montana).
- "I made a great decision in making our middle school principal the coordinator of our districtwide curriculum project. He has done a fine job" (Idaho).

## Accomplishment 4: Hiring or Firing Personnel

- "I've traveled over 200 miles a week during the last month to recruit teachers, and I'm pleased with the new teachers we have hired" (Minnesota).
- "I think I've done a good job of helping our principals get rid of ineffective teachers. That's a hard task in this district" (Tennessee).
- "I'm pleased with how our board and teachers' association came together to agree on an early retirement package. It will help us right away to get some new blood, while also reducing our budget in the short run" (Missouri).

Virtually all superintendents, except those in certain New Mexico and Arkansas districts with substantial federal impact funds, were preoccupied with bonds, budgets, and buildings, because the tenuous economies of the majority of districts we visited had been weakened seriously during the 1980s. One Michigan superintendent, for example, had just issued pink slips to 13 teachers, 4 of whom had taught in the district for eight years, while an Arizona-based superintendent, who served a district in a county with 35% unemployment, summed up what at least 14 other superintendents were thinking when he said that his greatest accomplishment had been "district survival."

Collaborative superintendents, more than the 14 others, were proud of having established a strengthened management team, improved attitudes of students toward school, renewed trust between the board and teachers, enhanced staff involvement in districtwide change, and increased cooperation with neighboring districts. More than their collaborative and laissez-faire counterparts, the 11 one-on-one superintendents were proud of bringing success to athletics, making their staffs more accountable, and designing a brand-new computer system for the district office. One of the one-on-one superintendents was proud of the cost savings he had brought about with the elimination of secretaries in the elementary schools.

## CHALLENGES THE SUPERINTENDENTS FACED

The superintendents told us they would continue to be challenged by many of the same types of things that they had accomplished, particularly with tight budgets during these hard times. They said they also would have difficulty getting bonds passed that had been previously voted down, and they would encounter frustration in hiring, transferring, and firing personnel and in encouraging instructional improvement in their schools. They also described some additional challenges during the 1990s.

### Challenge 1: Responding to State Mandates and Reform Reports

- "Our governor has made a name for himself by emphasizing education. The pressures for school improvement are tremendous in this state. The last few months, alone, I've been called to the capitol four times for special meetings on some aspect of educational excellence" (Tennessee).

- "Our State Department now requires us to use some form of Hunter's ITIP in evaluating teachers. That's meant that the principals and I have had to learn how to use ITIP. Its use has been causing a lot of tension among the teachers" (Texas).
- "The paperwork we have to do for the state continues to increase. Some weeks I spend virtually all my time on reports to the State Department. It's bad for small districts like ours, because we don't have staff, and I already ask my principals to do too many things" (Minnesota).

## Challenge 2: Raising Student Achievement Scores

- "Accountability is the theme these days, and student achievement is the bottom line. That's every educator's most serious challenge" (Iowa).
- "Test scores on student achievement are published in the newspapers, allowing for comparisons between districts in the state. That puts a lot of pressure on us to look good" (Wisconsin).
- "We're just starting now to do our achievement testing for the year. Tests are given to students in the fourth, sixth, eighth, and tenth grades. We feel pressure to improve our district scores from one testing period to the next" (Idaho).

## Challenge 3: Wrestling With Alcohol Abuse Among Secondary Students

- "A few years ago we had a terrible automobile accident here, in which four very popular students were killed. The driver had been drinking too much. That accident upset the community, and we've been working hard to control alcohol use among our students ever since" (Montana).
- "It's very hard to keep our seniors from drinking on the weekends, when their parents drink too much themselves on the weekend" (Arizona).

- "Last week we had a sophomore who brought a bottle of whiskey to school. Three of his friends drank most of the bottle between classes. We had to send them all home. It was a mess" (Wisconsin).

## Challenge 4: Coping With Asbestos, Lead, and Radon

- "This asbestos problem really hit us hard. We had to spend a considerable amount of money to get rid of some of it, or to thoroughly seal off the rest. I'm not sure we are out of the woods yet, because the state hasn't sent out the inspector yet" (Michigan).
- "It sounds funny, but I've had to spend a considerable amount of time dealing with the possibility that the drinking water in two of our older schools has lead in it" (California).
- "The latest issue is radon. It blows my mind. Now we might have to spend money to test for radon in our schools, and I don't believe that the state will give us money to do it" (Washington).

## Challenge 5: Helping Small, Country Schools to Survive

- "We're working hard to keep our small, country school, but enrollments are going down so I'm just not sure how much longer it will be able to survive" (Mississippi).
- "This will be the last year for our two-room elementary school 35 miles out in the country. Those kids will be bussed into town next year. Our decision wasn't at all popular with the families who live out there" (Michigan).
- "We're determined to maintain our two tiny country schools. We cut costs considerably when one principal took both schools" (Wisconsin).

The collaborative superintendents, more than the others, strove to improve the social climate of the district for both the educators and the students. They were more "people centered" in their thinking. One of the most inspirational and articulate of them, an Arizona-based superintendent, spoke about the need to reach out more to expand the K-12 focus of the district to include much more adult education, particularly education about effective parenting, as he commented, to "make the school for everybody in the community." His view, however, was atypical even for most of the other collaborative superintendents.

What was typical, unfortunately, was that most superintendents did not seem to be thinking much about curriculum and instruction. Curriculum development, for instance, was emphasized by only three superintendents, all of them collaborative. Aside from concern about how best to use ITIP for top-down supervision, only two superintendents indicated concern about instructional improvement. Equal educational opportunity for minorities, too, was not a salient issue for most superintendents, except in cases where there had been a recent discrimination case in the state or region. And concerns about teachers' participation in districtwide problem solving was rare.

The small-district superintendents we studied were different than their urban and suburban counterparts in at least three ways. First, the small-district superintendents were not preoccupied with intergroup or interpersonal conflict as were the superintendents portrayed, for example, in Blumberg's *The School Superintendent: Living With Conflict* (1985) or Cuban's *Urban School Chiefs Under Fire* (1976). Second, the superintendents we studied had to be generalists. They often were the only professional educator in the district office, and they had to be a jack-of-all-trades. Third, small-district superintendents were highly visible, public figures in their communities. Although their public relations strategies differed considerably from district to district, and some superintendents were more visible in town than others, they all played the single most important, public role in their communities.

## SUPERINTENDENTS' VIEWS ABOUT GENDER EQUITY

Along with our interest of 25 years in group processes and organization development, we have also had a serious, long-term interest in gender equity in schools. Our interest has focused on gender equity in school administration (P. Schmuck, 1982; Stockard et al., 1980), among educators internationally (P. Schmuck, 1987), and in the school and classroom (P. Schmuck, 1985; P. Schmuck & R. Schmuck, 1986). During the decade of the 1980s, we found that, while many educators became more aware of sexual discrimination and particular suburban and urban districts were making progress in reducing it, gender inequities were still omnipresent in our schools. We wondered about the status of gender equity in small districts.

We decided before our tour started to ask superintendents about their views about gender equity and what their districts were doing, if anything, to reduce or eliminate historical inequities between boys and girls. After our very first interview of a superintendent in California whom we found clearly wanting to eliminate gender inequities, we decided to include queries about equity in our subsequent interviews with principals and assistant principals to see whether they agreed with their superintendents.

We focused our inquiry on the superintendents' compliance with and their attitudes toward Title IX, the federal civil rights regulation that addressed equal access of girls and boys to all aspects of the school's program. After nearly two decades of national attention and public discussion on gender inequities in schools, we expected we would see not only some sensitivity to equal educational opportunities for boys and girls but also some concrete effects of Title IX. We looked for indications of integration or segregation by sex, of equal or unequal access by girls and boys to instructional programs and to extracurricular activities, and of more subtle signs of gender stereotyping. We said to the superintendents, "Tell us how your district provides equal educational opportunities for girls and boys" and then probed for specific examples. We asked principals about opportunities in their schools. We also inspected bulletin boards, studied written school policies, recorded classroom interaction, and observed students at play, in the halls, and during meals.

In their compliance with Title IX, we categorized the 25 superintendents into three stages: *denial of the issue* (5), *belief in full compliance* (10), and *actual compliance accompanied by concerns* (10).

## Denial of the Issue

Five superintendents, one laissez-faire and four one-on-one, thought that gender inequities were not an issue in their districts. They used words like "unimportant," "irrelevant," and "frivolous" to describe Title IX. They viewed our interest in equal educational opportunity for girls and boys as "academic," "theoretical," and even "stupid."

Those five superintendents, it appeared to us, were failing to do what they were getting paid to do. Their districts were receiving state and federal funds, and they were therefore legally obligated to comply with state and federal directives. Nevertheless, they were not complying with Title IX, nor did they intend to comply. Indeed, three of the five appeared red in the face and physically agitated when we raised the question. We later corroborated the superintendents' denial of the issue through interviews with their principals and by our observations. For example, we did not find as many sports activities for girls as for boys, and we did not find as many girls as boys in the advanced math and science classes at the high schools, but the principals did not see those facts as indicators of inequity.

A middle school principal in Arizona told us, "That stuff about our treating boys and girls differently is stupid. I don't believe it. It's just that girls don't want to do the same things as boys when they get to high school. Our teachers here teach kids; I don't care if they are boys or girls. They are all just kids." But that principal's defensiveness was more emotional than most others, who completely denied the issue. Most of the principals in those five districts simply could not see a problem. An elementary principal in Illinois quickly said, "We don't do anything special to attract girls to math and computers or boys to reading and writing. We just treat everyone the same." Another elementary principal in that same district said, "I tell the teachers when I supervise to mix up whom you call upon, but I never even thought of watching to see if they call on girls and boys equally." And a high school principal in Arizona could see "no issue since boys and girls participate in the same activities. We all ride the same bus, eat the same food, go to the same classes; so there's just not a lot of difference."

Our further investigation of those five districts indicated that they were not complying with Title IX. Their policy handbooks and board minutes did not mention Title IX, nor did they set forth any grievance procedures for redressing unequal educational opportunities. There were fewer sports offerings for girls than for boys and there were very few girls in higher-level math and science classes. We saw girls being used as office assistants and boys as safety guards at street corners; bulletin boards showcasing important men in history; and, in four classes, teachers behaving toward students in sex-stereotyped ways such as lining up girls and boys in segregated lines, calling only on boys to move heavy objects, and asking only girls to run errands outside the classroom. We saw no indication that the superintendents or principals we interviewed were offering any leadership whatsoever to encourage teachers to reduce gender inequities.

## Belief in Full Compliance

Ten superintendents, two laissez-faire, six one-on-one, and two collaborative, reported that they had eliminated discriminatory behavior both in their instructional programs and in their extracurricular activities. A Washington superintendent told us, "We have no sex discrimination here. We know we must have the same or equivalent activities for girls and boys, and we do." A superintendent in Iowa said, "There was an idea 20 years ago when I became an administrator that girls should do certain things and that boys should do other things. Today that idea has changed; now girls can do everything boys can do." A superintendent in Idaho believed that "all compliance efforts with Title IX have been realized. Unequivocally no one is denied anything by gender in this district. If we have any problems at all, I haven't heard about them from the principals, the teachers, the parents, or the students."

By and large, our observations and subsequent interviews corroborated the superintendents' views. There was equal access to opportunities in those districts, and most of the principals sought to eliminate overt discrimination in their schools. A few principals denied the issue entirely, but most were seriously striving to comply with the letter of the law in Title IX. Girls and boys had the same number of school-sponsored sports; they both were given similar vocational opportunities ranging from cooking to woodworking, and girls were being recruited into the advanced math and science courses. In the elementary schools, girls and boys were being largely integrated in waiting lines, and bulletin boards offered the work of girls and boys and the societal achievements of women and men.

What set these 10 districts off, however, from our next category of districts was the administrators' apparent lack of concern in working on reducing the more subtle forms of discrimination. For example, we did not observe teachers teaching lessons about gender discrimination in the world, nor did we find administrators really encouraging students and parents to put as much emphasis on girls' sports as boys' sports. Football, boys' basketball, and hockey were major community events. Boys were the featured stars; girls contributed window dressing through cheerleading and cheering the boys on from the stands. In the elementary schools, we saw boys getting more feedback from teachers than girls, and girls less frequently being reprimanded than boys. And it was rare to find a male primary teacher in these 10 districts.

## Full Compliance With Concerns

Ten superintendents, one one-on-one and nine collaborative, reported that, although their districts were complying with Title IX, they continued to be perplexed over how to satisfy the "spirit of the law." A Mississippi-based superintendent told us, "Through the years we've tried in our vocational program to recruit boys and girls into nontraditional specialties. But today we have only two females in building trades, only one in autoshop, and none in mechanics. Clothing, on the other hand, has no boy. We try but we just don't make it."

In Minnesota, the superintendent and high school principal met together with us to chat about taking affirmative action to go beyond equal opportunity. They focused on what they referred to as "the tough interpersonal issues." The high school principal told us, "We've tried very hard to recruit girls into agriculture and autoshop, and our middle school has helped a lot because all vocational subjects there are required for boys and girls, but . . . the boys show off their chivalry and say, 'Here let me do that for you,' like greasing the axle or tightening a screw, and the girls let them because, I guess, they don't want grease under their fingernails or they don't want to appear stronger, or something. We can create access but actual equity is elusive."

Other superintendents reported frustration with the community's reaction to girls taking on nontraditional roles. A superintendent in New Mexico said, "I'm pleased with girls taking welding and boys taking sewing, but traditional roles are so ingrained in this community that there's a lot of pressure on girls especially to get ready to be housewives. Really, there's more pressure on boys and girls fitting into traditional roles from the parents than from the schools. We're working to cope with that pressure, but it's difficult. Primarily, we're trying to get our elementary and middle school teachers to stress gender equity in their classrooms."

All 10 of these districts offered the same number of sports for girls as for boys, but the question of girls playing football was an active issue in two of them. In one district, a junior girl made the football team but didn't play much "because she wasn't as skilled as the boys," according to the superintendent. He went on to say, "She would have been better off on the freshmen team, but she was a junior." In another district, a girl was playing on the offense. "I didn't like the idea at all, but I allowed her to do it," the superintendent told us. "Her parents visited with me and made a lot of valid points. They wanted her to be able to play if she could make the team. I came to respect her and her parents. We don't consciously stereotype, but of course it happens all the time. I've got a daughter, myself, and I want her to be able to do what she chooses." Indeed, we met six superintendents who were concerned that their own daughters would have the opportunity for many options in life.

The superintendents in this third category used words like "stereotyping," "prejudice," "bias," and "equity" in talking about complying with Title IX. Two talked about a district they knew of where a sex discrimination suit had been brought against the board. They were acutely aware of both the formal and the informal practices of discrimination. Four others were sponsoring workshops on gender equity in their districts, including "Gender Expectations and Student Achievement" (GESA) and "Teacher Expectations and Student Achievement" (TESA). A superintendent in Minnesota told us, "We say we don't discriminate, yet I'm sure we do. The idea of subtle bias and unconscious prejudice should get more attention here. Sure, we have open access, but I think we also have some responsibility for reducing stereotypes."

Compared with the 15 other districts, the 10 in which we found concern about gender discrimination had higher numbers of female principals and assistant principals, had more superintendents with a collaborative management style, had more workshops or conferences about gender equity, and were in states in which either prominent court cases or active auditing by the state department of education had raised the educators' awareness about gender discrimination in the schools.


## PORTRAITS OF FIVE SUPERINTENDENTS

We were impressed by the work of five collaborative superintendents in very different regions of the country. There was Ray Pugh in Missouri, who was working diligently to open the communication channels between the community and the teachers; Jamie Stowell in Mississippi, who was helping make racial desegregation work; Richard Maxwell in California, whose use of the management team was exemplary; Frank Rodriguez in Montana, who demonstrated effective meetings' skills; and Joseph Gomez in Arizona, who was inspiring the educators and students in his district to work hard to improve the academic program.


### Ray Pugh

When we met Ray Pugh on a rainy day in rural Missouri, he was busily working on the proposed budget for the next school year. Now at 52 years of age, Ray had been the superintendent of this small district for seven years. He was most proud of his efforts to keep communication open among teachers, administrators, and the board.

Six times a year, Ray Pugh convened a formal group, known by the acronym TAB (teachers, administrators, and board) to surface problems, share perceptions and feelings, and make recommendations. The TAB was made up of eight teachers (two from each of the district's four schools), two site administrators, and two board members. Membership was rotated from year to year, which made it possible for all administrators and board members to serve over a three-year period.

Pugh commenced each meeting by posing issues that had come to his attention and went on to elicit other topics from the members. Pugh told us, "I self-consciously plan these to be open-bitch sessions and usually we do have spirited exchanges and high involvement." He said that the last TAB meeting, which occurred only a week before our visit to the district, was "particularly engaging." That meeting had started at 5:30 p.m. and had lasted until midnight. Examples of issues discussed were (a) alcohol use among teenagers, (b) infrequent communication about curriculum between teachers at the two elementary schools, (c) slim offerings in vocational education, and (d) inaccurate communication between teachers at the junior high and high schools.

Although Pugh played down the effectiveness of TAB in our interview, it was the only example we found of a districtwide, formal group, with regular meetings and rotating membership, which discussed cross-district problems outside of collective bargaining. One board member lauded the TAB, stating, "I enjoy it more than anything I do as a board member. We discuss everything openly with the teachers from potholes in the driveway to pay increases." And the TAB also was serving as a model to others for surfacing problems. For example, we found in our interviews with two of the district's principals that both of them were trying out a similar procedure in each of their schools, by enlisting representatives from grade levels and subject matter specialties to serve on advisory groups. Like the TAB, those two school-based advisory groups met regularly and rotated memberships from year to year.

We agreed with Pugh's view that "advisory groups which meet in an atmosphere of openness and acceptance can contribute to the problem-solving ability of a district." Unfortunately, district problems were not being disclosed to many superintendents we met, particularly those with one-on-one and laissez-faire management styles, because they were not clearly stating through their actions that they wished to learn about them. Indeed, we saw at least 14 districts in which the principals acted as insulators between the superintendents and the problems felt by the teachers. Groups like the TAB, at the very least, can provide a legitimate avenue for surfacing district problems with the boss.

*Jamie Stowell*

In Mississippi, we met Jamie Stowell, who told us about an exemplary practice facilitated by a superintendent of the generation before, which Stowell felt was still having favorable effects today. The year before desegregation had to take place, by law, black and white administrators discussed how to make a smooth and effective transition. They convened meetings of parents and students from both the black and the white communities to discuss how the newly desegregated schools would operate.

"Later," Stowell related, "they brought together student leaders from the black and white schools in summer workshops to prepare a student handbook for the desegregated high school." A black principal of those days, now retired, told us, "We worked hard to get the black and white power structures together. We were fortunate in having a superintendent and board, both of which wanted to pull together. Of course, the students had to be involved. Students had to determine what type of school they wanted and the students had to know that there was no option. Integration would have to occur."

Stowell told us, "The district is still functioning effectively today. There has been no white flight and race relations in our schools are fine." We thought, along with Stowell, how much power there can be in bringing students into the planned changes that a district might be undergoing, from desegregation to new procedures for teacher evaluation or plans for a middle school or an alternative high school. Stowell was proud of his school district.

## Richard Maxwell

Maxwell was one of the few thoroughly collaborative superintendents in our sample. Although all 11 collaborative superintendents used regularly scheduled meetings with their principals, only one of the one-on-one superintendents did. The other 13 called for meetings with the principals only "when the need arises." Thus, for most of the superintendents we studied, the slogan that Maxwell displayed prominently on his desk was fitting: *The greatest problem with communication is the illusion that it has been achieved.*

The California-based Maxwell had been superintendent for four years. His experiences as a language disorders teacher, speech pathologist, director of compensatory education, and assistant superintendent had helped him develop a deep appreciation and concern for clear communication, egalitarian relationships, and participatory management. He was proud of having established a cohesive, nine-person management team, consisting of two assistant superintendents, the coordinator of special education, five principals, and himself.

In the room where the management team met, every two weeks for three or four hours, we noticed poster paper taped to the walls with information from the team's work. There were piles of articles, papers, and journals on a large table in the center of the room around which the team members would sit face-to-face. Every administrative concern about the district appeared to be appropriate for team deliberation, such as implementing board policies, distributing lottery funds, facing difficult personnel problems, developing teacher schedules, and building collaborative negotiations with the teachers' union. Agenda items came from each member, and each of them told us that Maxwell's meeting procedures were effective.

Maxwell told us, "Participatory management has always been a part of my background. I started it when I first got here, but it's taken four years to get it really going. First, I expressed my concern, over and over again, that I wanted all administrators to work as a team; second, I set up workshops, meetings, and procedures so we'd function like a team; and finally, after time, trust developed."

Maxwell added, "Right now, we are decentralizing decision making. The team just went through 200 items deciding who decides, what principals could decide on their own, or jointly and so on. We are trying to clarify for everyone just what school-based management means in a small district. We still have a long way to go."

### Frank Rodriguez

Frank Rodriguez, a superintendent in Montana, ran perhaps the most effective meeting that we observed on the tour. Overall, we found that, of the 12 superintendents who employed scheduled meetings, only 5 clearly demonstrated effective meetings' procedures, that is, offered a clear and detailed agenda before the meeting, used group convening and communication skills, and assigned a recorder to summarize results of the meeting. Ray Pugh and Robert Maxwell were two of them, but Frank Rodriguez was the best.

We observed Rodriguez chairing an administrative team meeting at the district office. Present were four principals, one assistant principal, the business manager, a specialist in special education, and Rodriguez. The eight sat around a small table, so, physically, they were quite close to one another. Rodriguez had mailed out an agenda a few days before and had called each member to make sure he or she was clear about the agenda and would be attending the meeting. Virtually every member spoke during the discussion of each agenda item. Rodriguez frequently paraphrased the statements of others and, before going on to the next agenda item, checked for approval from every member to move ahead. Twice decisions were called for; both times, every individual was surveyed for his or her point of view. Once, we observed a member's contribution being ignored, but that member did finally get the point across later in the meeting. Toward the end of the meeting, Rodriguez asked one of the principals, who was assigned the role of recorder, to summarize the decisions made during the meeting. After the meeting was over, Rodriguez and the recorder met to review the minutes. It was the only meeting we had seen in six months that was efficient and effective. The administrative team had truly communicated in an I-Thou fashion while also accomplishing a great deal.

## Joseph Gomez

Joseph Gomez, one of only four Hispanic superintendents in Arizona in 1989, exemplified many of the attributes of an instructional leader. Very visible and charming to the students, teachers, principals, and an 85% Hispanic community, he seemed to be everywhere, from eating breakfast with students to directing traffic with the chief custodian at the end of the school day. During the school day, he practiced "management by walking around"; with the limitless energy of a 42-year-old (the youngest in our sample) who was in excellent condition, Gomez was visible in the halls, the lunchroom, the classes, and the athletic fields.

When he had become superintendent 10 years previously at the young age of 32, Gomez inherited what he called "a mess." In his words, "the students were rude and undisciplined, the curriculum was old fashioned and not progressive, and the school did not belong to the community." He went on to say, "The old guard superintendent was too powerful; school did not belong to the community but to the superintendent. He was the expert and everyone respected him. He was *the* schools. I believe in local control and have worked to return the schools to the parents."

He set out to replace undisciplined students' behavior with school pride and student self-esteem, an outmoded curriculum with one more up to date, and an apathetic and alienated community with a community-school program. Although, because of very poor economic conditions in the town, he faced an uphill climb, it appeared that he was making significant progress in renewing the schools.

Gomez had been putting a personal touch on most everything. Frequently smiling during informal conversation with everyone who came along, he manifested respect and interest in others while maintaining humility and a sense of humor. He had visited homes and churches to encourage more parent participation in the schools. He had sought personal relationships with many students to give them a sense of pride in their school, their town, and themselves. He had empowered parents by giving them important responsibilities in the schools, such as being playground monitors, teacher aides, kitchen assistants, and tutors for individual students. He had initiated a curriculum overhaul in the basic skills and kept it going by bringing the principals and teachers together through a curriculum needs assessment and by bringing in consultants to help teachers' committees to develop new curricula. He also had been meeting regularly for seven years with his administrative team to solve districtwide problems.

## TARGETS OF CHANGE

Like Ravel's solo trumpeter, it is up to the superintendent, alone, to herald, loud and clear, the idea that small-district schools should be for everybody. In his creative way, Ray Pugh proclaimed that theme by establishing and nurturing the TAB. Jamie Stowell did that, too, by retelling the inspirational story, not only to us but to the citizens of his town, of how black and white administrators of the generation before had drawn student leaders into the racial integration of the high school. Richard Maxwell enacted the theme, in part, by initiating and supporting administrative teamwork, and Frank Rodriguez played out the theme in microcosm within a single team meeting. Joseph Gomez trumpeted the theme over and over again by taking part in I-Thou exchanges with students, teachers, administrators, parents, and citizens at large. He did play first trumpet, so to speak, in the community.

Now, we go beyond what we saw on tour to describe other actions that small-district superintendents might take to lead their communities toward more humane transactions in the schools.

### Superintendents in Relation to Principals

To establish an interdependent and cohesive administrative team is an important target that small-district superintendents should announce loud and clear. They should embrace the concepts and techniques of organization development (OD) as a daily mode of operation. OD is a planned and sustained effort at system transformation in which the members of the system themselves continually diagnose, act, and evaluate events and action to improve their own organization. It entails self-conscious, deliberate, and collaborative problem solving among the members of an administrative team.

Superintendents must take on a less traditional, nonhierarchical role if they are to perform effectively as conveners of problem solving. Benevolence and warm paternalism are no longer virtues. Rather, empathic understanding will be required, along with a willingness to enter into uncomfortable disagreements and to settle them amicably. The communication skills of paraphrasing, describing behavior objectively, describing one's own feelings directly, checking impressions of another's feelings, summarizing, compromising, and reducing tension are important to establish constructive openness among the principals during their problem-solving discussions. Unilateral decision making is not usually appropriate, but openness about one's own feelings engendered by the role of superintendent is needed to strengthen trust with the principals.

When principals of small districts are confronted with a superintendent's leadership that is at variance with what they expect, it is understandable that the principals should feel some distrust toward the superintendent. Much of principals' management experiences have taught them not only that the authority in small districts does not behave democratically but that the teamwork espoused by the head is more hierarchical than egalitarian. Our interpretation of the behavior of many principals is that they might initially respond to a collaborative superintendent as a phoney or as "playing a game" to protect themselves from the risks implicit in engaging with the superintendent on more democratic terms. It is therefore critical for the superintendent taking a new, collaborative role to persist in the collaborative stance over a long period of time to gain the confidence and trust of the principals.

*Consensus decision making.* Group consensus is a decision-making method especially appropriate for the small, face-to-face administrative team. All participants contribute their thoughts and feelings and all share in the final decisions. No decision becomes final that is not understood by nearly all members. But consensus does *not* mean that all agree. It means that (a) all can paraphrase the issue to show they understand it; (b) all have a chance to describe their feelings about the issue; and (c) those who continue to disagree will nevertheless say publicly that they are willing to give the decision an experimental try for a prescribed period of time. In other words, consensus means that a sufficient number of team members are in favor of a decision and will not obstruct its implementation.

Decision making by consensus does not happen by intention only; it will require skill in two-way communication, in coping with conflict, in the use of paraphrasing, and in surveying the opinions within the team. When an administrative team is capable of performing those skills, consensus decision making can increase the team's effectiveness for three reasons. First, because creative ideas of team members might remain untapped when one-way communication predominates, consensus decision making allows for more public pooling of the knowledge, insights, and personal choices of team members. Second, consensus decision making facilitates team effectiveness especially when the knowledge and insights about an issue are shared by many within the team—a phenomenon that is typical of highly complex educational issues. And, third, consensus decision making increases the likelihood of committed implementation of a decision because everyone has been engaged in the final decision.

Thus consensus decision making can increase an administrative team's effectiveness, both by enhancing the quality of its problem solving and by increasing members' commitment to the implementation of the team's decisions. It will be especially effective when an administrative team faces complex issues with many alternative subtasks, when the elements of the issue are not easily conceptualized, and, in particular, when efficient execution of a decision depends on the continued coordination and interaction of a number of teammates.

*Diagnosis of district effectiveness.* The administrative team should self-consciously and continually diagnose the strengths and shortcomings of the district's schools. Before focusing on teachers and students, however, the administrative team should diagnose its own effectiveness. And, before focusing on the group dynamics of the team itself, the superintendent should initiate within the team a diagnosis of his or her role as a collaborative leader. As an initial step, superintendents might ask the principals to respond anonymously on an open-ended questionnaire to questions such as the following: "For us to establish a trusting and cohesive administrative team, what are some things that I should

(a) keep doing *the same*?
(b) start doing *more often*?
(c) start doing *less often*?"

Next, the superintendent should analyze the principals' responses, searching for themes that recur in answers to each of the three questions. Later, the superintendent should tell the principals about the results and suggest a few things that he or she will attempt to do more often and a few things that he or she will attempt to do less often. Some weeks after that, the superintendent should find out from the principals how he or she is doing in an attempt to establish a trusting and cohesive administrative team.

Superintendents who commence self-conscious diagnosis of district effectiveness with themselves are demonstrating through their own actions that improvement should be the district's goal at all system levels. In turn, the superintendent's requests for diagnoses of the administrative team, of the principals as viewed by their teachers, and of the teachers as viewed by students and parents will be viewed by all as more legitimate if their superintendent has previously put him- or herself on the line. Note too that superintendents who initiate these *upward evaluations* are breaking from the traditional supervisory procedure in school districts of downward evaluation.

*The importance of ego strength.* Perhaps the most important personal attribute needed by small-district superintendents is ego strength. Ego strength in leading means that superintendents possess clear values and an internal gyroscope that helps maintain their direction toward a goal. It also means that they frequently state publicly their hopes, aspirations, and goals for the district. Moreover, strong superintendents let the principals know early during team building what decisions will be the superintendent's and what decisions will be the administrative team's. For example, if superintendents intend to maintain veto power over budget decisions or control over the board agenda, they should strongly discourage team discussion about those matters. On the other hand, if superintendents wish to receive input from the principals about the budget or board agenda, they should clearly state that they want advice but the final decisions will be theirs. Superintendents with ego strength do not have hidden agendas, nor do they set out deliberately to manipulate a principal into thinking as they do.

Strength in leading means that superintendents relinquish their traditional power honestly and patiently. It means that they stimulate the imagination of the principals through their own excitement and enthusiasm, and it means that they energize and systematize the team's problem solving and decision making. Frequently, such collaborative and democratic leadership leads to uncomfortable interactions and to difficult interpersonal confrontations. Ego strength in leading means that superintendents expect conflicts to arise and that they do not carry defensiveness from those uncomfortable interactions once they have been worked through.

## Superintendents in Relation to Students

Three student-oriented themes should be trumpeted by small-district superintendents: (a) The goal of education is to help individual students develop so that they might become self-confident, productive citizens of a democracy. (b) The challenge of educators is to uncover students' thoughts and feelings about school life. (c) The task of educators is to use that student information to upgrade the school's curriculum and instruction. In other words, the educator's role is to serve students, and, by listening to their inner voices, the educators will be better able to create teaching strategies to facilitate students' development.

Small-district superintendents themselves should initiate discussions with students to demonstrate that they indeed are serious about wishing to listen to students. A few years ago, we consulted with a California-based superintendent in a district of about 5,000 students, who held biweekly formal meetings with student council members from the district's two high schools. They discussed aspects of high school life that the students liked and aspects that they hoped could be changed. The superintendent asked the students, at each school, to meet together for 30 minutes, before he arrived, so that they would have time alone to make two lists, for "things we'd like to stay the same" and "things we'd like to see changed." He would spend about 45 minutes at each school to go over the content of the lists with the students from that school. He probed the students particularly for examples of their complaints and dislikes.

Later, he would bring some of the student data to the district's once-a-week administrative team meetings. He was careful to accentuate the strengths of each school to the principals and to keep the number and emotional tone of the dislikes equal between the schools. All district principals plus the superintendent and assistant superintendent then brainstormed actions that could be carried out to make changes on issues of concern to students. The superintendent did not encourage the team to make decisions about the proposed action ideas; rather, he told the high school principals that it would be up to them to use any ideas they thought might work in their respective schools.

In another instance, after we had published a journal article about our student data from the tour, in the *Bulletin of the National Association of Secondary School Principals* in 1991, we received a letter from a small-district superintendent in Eastern Oregon, in which he praised us for the idea that educators should listen more carefully to student concerns. He went on to tell us that he would be presenting our findings to the principals and teachers of his district at a daylong in-service workshop in June. He planned to ask the educators in his district to pinpoint teachers' behaviors, and those of principals, that turn off students. His guess was that they would list things like "in a bad mood," "humorless," "frowning," "putdowns," and "never calls on me for help"; behaviors very similar to those the students told us about in our interviews. He hoped that such disclosures at the in-service event would motivate the principals and teachers to act more sensitively and empathically toward students.

Both of those superintendents demonstrated in their own ways that they were willing to act publicly on their beliefs that schools exist to serve students and that student opinions about school should be heeded by teachers and principals. On tour, we met a superintendent in Iowa who had facilitated the placement of student representatives on the school board. Other ways that superintendents might bring students into important aspects of school life were described in Chapter 2, that is, as participants in the selection and assessment of teachers and as contributors to community development. The particular activity is not the issue. In the main, small-district superintendents should seek to create avenues whereby student voices can be heard by educators in the district. As a start, superintendents might attempt to accomplish that themselves by holding formal advisory sessions with students and by regularly visiting the schools to talk informally with students.

## Superintendents in Relation to Teachers

We have consulted in a medium-sized district near Portland, Oregon, in which the superintendent had observed every teacher in the classroom for at least 30 minutes during one school year. That district had 382 teachers, and he watched and talked personally with every single one of them. At the end of the academic year, even as collective bargaining was tense between teacher negotiators and the board, the district teacher association paid for a special dinner to honor and praise the superintendent for getting to all of the district's classroom teachers. A few weeks later, at a statewide professional meeting of school administrators, we saw a few administrators from that district wearing specially designed T-shirts that read:

Those who can,
TEACH.
Those who can't
go into some less
significant line of work.

Let us assume that our teacher-oriented superintendent had 38 weeks to visit classrooms. That would mean he would have had to visit about 10 teachers per week or, on the average, 2 per day. Compare his challenge with that of the small-district superintendents we visited. The largest of the districts on our tour had around 100 teachers, which means that the superintendents would have had to see fewer than 3 teachers per week to observe all of them once per year. Most of the superintendents in our study could have observed all of their teachers in action by getting to 2 per week.

Although it is possible that we missed getting that information, we doubt sincerely that the small-district superintendents in our sample were on a schedule to observe in every classroom during a single year. Joseph Gomez, the best of our superintendents, might have visited every classroom teacher over the course of a few years, but we doubt that any of the 25 observed and talked personally with every teacher about a specific lesson in a single academic year. Moreover, except for Gomez and Maxwell, it was rare for us to find superintendents who publicly provided encouragement to their teachers. And nowhere did we find T-shirts as clever as those worn by the administrators in our home state of Oregon.

As we have delineated previously in this chapter, we realize that small-district superintendents are overloaded with myriad, relatively trivial, noneducational tasks that the superintendents of larger districts can delegate or simply avoid. It is, however, very important for small-district superintendents to champion the idea that the most important educators in the district are the teachers. Although schools exist for student growth and development, teachers are the key adults for unlocking the students' potential. The superintendent should be their staunchest ally and cheerleader. Superintendents should attempt not only to visit every teacher for at least 30 minutes per year but also to get to meetings of teams, departments, and staffs to articulate over and over again how absolutely crucial supportive teacher-student relationships are to the well-being of the school and the community.


### Superintendents in Relation to Community

Much more than their metropolitan counterparts, small-district superintendents are on center stage in their communities. After superintendents have been in office for a few weeks, most everyone in the community knows who they are and often has had opportunities to talk with them, on the streets, at the grocery, at church, or in the restaurant. Indeed, the superintendent and the high school principal are two of the best known public figures in small communities all over the western United States.

The trumpet theme we would like to see small-town superintendents play for their community is that, for education to be effective these days, the entire community will have to play a part; everyone will have to contribute. Yes, it is proper for the school to be the entertainment center of the community; but it is even more important for the school to be the education center of the community. Education is for everyone from preschoolers to those in their senior years, and teaching and learning should be available to everyone.

Superintendents should present a vision of the value of teaching and learning for everyone in the community. A vehicle for getting adults to come to the school as teachers and learners could be, for example, computer clubs in which people of all ages can act both as teachers and as learners. Another vehicle is the reading circle in which books are read, reported on, and discussed by people with common interests. Another vehicle is tutoring: Adults can volunteer time to tutor adolescents in exchange for some personal growth or parenting seminars presented by experts at the school. Superintendents themselves could take part in one or two of those educational activities to show their support for the concept that education is appropriate and relevant at all ages.

Superintendents of small districts should deliberately step forward as community leaders—to become the educational leaders of their communities. They should appear at meetings of the businesses, the grange, the service clubs, and the churches to solicit support for lifelong education in the community. We are not thinking here about economic support but psychological support and citizens' commitment to participate as teachers and learners in the educational culture of the community. Although superintendents must trumpet inspirational messages about the value of everyone becoming committed to lifelong education, their distinct solo presentations should, if their leadership is successful, fade into the unitary blend of a full orchestral crescendo of community members participating in the academic life of the school.

## REFERENCES

Blumberg, A. (1985). *The school superintendent: Living with conflict.* New York: Teachers College Press.

Carlson, R. O. (1970). The adoption of educational innovations. In M. B. Miles & W. W. Charters, Jr. (Eds.), *Learning in social settings* (pp. 672-689). Boston: Allyn & Bacon.

Cuban, L. (1976). *Urban school chiefs under fire.* Chicago: University of Chicago Press.

Cuban, L. (1988). *The managerial imperative and the practice of leadership in schools.* Albany: State University of New York Press.

Gross, N., Mason, W., & McEachern, A. (1958). *Explorations in role analysis.* New York: John Wiley.

Schmuck, P. (1982). *Sex equity in educational leadership: The Oregon story.* Newton, MA: Educational Development Corporation.

Schmuck, P. (1985). Administrative strategies to implement sex equity. In *Handbook for achieving sex equity through education.* Baltimore: Johns Hopkins Press.

Schmuck, P. (1987). *Women educators: Employees of schools in Western countries.* Albany: State University of New York Press.

Schmuck, P., & Schmuck, R. (1986). How schools sustain sex-role inequities: An outline for a program of action research. In E. Wallin, M. Soderstrom, & G. Borg (Eds.), *Educational research and organization theory* (Vol. 2). Uppsala, Sweden: University of Uppsala.

Schmuck, R., & Schmuck, P. (1991, March). The attitudes of adolescents in small town America. *Bulletin of the National Association of Secondary School Principals*, pp. 85-95.

Stockard, J., Schmuck, P., Kempner, K., Williams, P., Edson, S., & Smith, M. A. (1980). *Sex equity in education.* New York: Academic Press.

Wissler, D. F., & Ortiz, F. I. (1988). *The superintendent's leadership in school reform.* New York: Falmer.

# 6

▲
⊔

## School Boards

### FORGING LINKS TO
### PARENTS AND COMMUNITY

In the broad and final sense all institutions are educational in
the sense that they operate to form the attitudes, dispositions,
abilities and disabilities that constitute a concrete personality.
The principle applies with special force to the school. For it
is the main business of the family and the school to influence
directly the formation and growth of attitudes and dispositions, emotional, intellectual and moral. Whether this educa-
tive process is carried on in a predominately democratic or
non-democratic way becomes, therefore, a question of tran-
scendent importance not only for education itself but for its
final effect upon all the interests and activities of a society
that is committed to a democratic way of life.

*—John Dewey, 1916, quoted in Ratner, 1939, p. 717*

Having resided in Western Oregon for nearly half our lives, we have
grown to appreciate the rain. It furnishes the Cascades with snow

141

that melts to irrigate our fertile valleys, cleanses the polluted air in
our atmosphere, bathes the roots of our elegant rhododendrons, and
produces a green terrain so stunningly brilliant that it can hurt one's
eyes. Although meteorologists inform us that Eugene truly receives
the same quantity of annual rainfall as Philadelphia, the Oregon mist
has always seemed to us to persist infinitely longer than the Pennsylvania downpours.

Thus, when we reviewed our tour, one month before departure,
from the faraway confines of a poorly heated room in frigid China,
we anticipated that the weather on our forthcoming route—south in
winter, north in spring—would be mostly sunny and dry compared
with the gray, wet winters and springs in the Willamette Valley.
Ironically, we seemed to bring the Oregon rain to drought-stricken
America. Of the 160 days we traveled, rain or snow fell on 85 of
them. We estimated, overall, an accumulation of 23 inches of rain
and 17 inches of snow on our tour. In fact, we encountered rain or
snow in every state, even in Southern Arizona. In Texas alone, we
received more than four inches of cold rain in less than three weeks
and, as we motored west across the northern tier of states, we braved
rain or snow throughout April, May, and June.

In early May, after two days of intermittent snow flurries and
dismal skies, with signs of spring at last becoming visible on the
great plains, we walked from our RV park to a school board meeting
in a community in the heartland of North Dakota. Chaste white birch
trees sprayed light green leaves against a vast blue sky, and tall grain
elevators stood majestically against the firmament upon an unending
horizon. Would spring be here at last?

Five school board members, all of whom greeted us warmly and
enthusiastically, were quick to tell us about their frustration and
commitment in serving a district with citizens who, at times, seemed
all too unappreciative. Like other board members we had met previously, and like the inclement weather we had encountered, these
North Dakotans' optimistic thoughts about their dedicated efforts on
behalf of the community were overcast with gloomy, gray feelings
of discouragement.

We met Jerry Baker, who became a teacher in a community next
door to the one in which he was born. Baker told us that, although

he had enjoyed teaching, he found that he could better support four children by driving for the United Parcel Service at twice the pay of a teacher. We met Donald Unser, who had attended a nearby, one-room country school, now closed, went to college for two years, then went to the military for four, and finally returned home to run his parents' farm. We met Ginnie Carson, who had moved around her whole life as a "military brat" and finally settled on her grand-parents' centennial farm. And we met two other men who also had been raised locally: Sam Dunn was a building maintenance manager at a local hospital, while David Zander, after spending 10 years away, had returned to manage his parents' farm. Their stories of returning home again to the small community were similar to the life histories of other board members with whom we spoke in the small districts of western America.

The five of them, along with the superintendent, two principals, and a school secretary, sat about a large square table in the teachers' lounge of the high school. Coffee and cookies were served as they greeted one another warmly with friendly jokes and hearty laughter. They were soon ready to work and the board meeting started on time at 7:30 p.m. Observers of the meeting included two special education teachers, the local newspaper editor, and the two of us.

The first agenda item focused on an elementary school student with a learning disability. The two special education teachers, available as consultants to the board, gave their assessments of the student's problem. After lengthy discussion during which all five board members actively took part, the superintendent, the two visiting teachers, and the board agreed unanimously to provide pedagogical services outside the school district at considerable cost to the district. The decision was complicated; it required information, time, and reflection and displayed the caring concerns for students of the board members.

The second agenda item dealt with bus transportation. The superintendent brought to the table a map of the district pasted to a large piece of beige cardboard and said, "We have the Englishes and the Packards to pick up here," while he pointed to the map. "If the Farrahs move to town next year, we will be able to save about 10 minutes. I've got to talk to Sam in the County office. He says that this road here won't be fixed for another few years. I think three of those families should have their last kids graduating this year, so maybe we don't have to worry." Unser and Carson asked questions for clarification but no decision was required. The superintendent was merely informing the board of changes in bus routes that could occur in the future. As Jerry Baker told us, "Parents of school children in rural areas tend to be protective and outspoken about their children's bus routes."

From our vantage point, that North Dakota board demonstrated competence, conscientiousness, and civic responsibility. It presented a living portrait of representative democracy in action and of the sort of local problem solving that can go on monthly in school districts throughout the United States. The agenda was about improving the quality of life for a 10-year-old girl with special needs and trouble-shooting the mundane but inevitable problems of the ubiquitous yellow school bus.

We were impressed by Baker, Carson, Dunn, Unser, and Zander. We were struck by the quality of the questions raised and by the thoroughness of the responses offered by the teachers and administrators. We were strongly affected, too, by how well the board members listened to one another and how efficiently they made a decision. We commented to each other, after the meeting, about how conscientiously those five lay people had taken responsibility for a disabled child. Whereas only two decades ago, the parents of that little girl would have had to take the primary responsibility for educating her, now five citizens were helping make decisions about the quality of her special education, indeed the quality of her life. It was an impressive demonstration of how the statute known as 94-142 can alter responsibility and morality in the ways our schools serve the citizenry. And the problems of school buses, such as whether the Farrahs will move and save the bus driver 10 minutes, are omnipresent in small districts.

All over America, small-district boards deal continually with issues ranging from at-risk and learning disabled youngsters to bus transportation. Both morality and logistics, the sublime and the mundane, are the business of school boards today. In this chapter, we focus on our observations and interviews of 28 small-district school board members. On tour, we sought to describe the sorts of challenges that boards were struggling with, their irksome problems and difficult dilemmas. We also searched for exemplary practices that would be worthwhile communicating to others.

## THE CHANGING ECONOMY OF SMALL COMMUNITIES

The demographic characteristics of the small districts we visited had changed from a generation ago, because of continual migration into Sunbelt cities and a precipitous economic decline in the rural United States. Whereas once small American communities housed stable and securely rooted citizens, during the last 10 years they have attracted many uprooted and transient people, like the Joads, looking for inexpensive housing and special services. Although a few rural areas are growing in the West, many small communities today are in severe economic jeopardy. Mineral deposits have been mined, family farms have been purchased by corporations, labor-intensive agriculture has become mechanized, less and less timber has been available for cutting, and many small industries have been forced to shut down. With reduced employment opportunities, fewer people have had the money to spend in small communities, and therefore the small service businesses too have had to close.

A pointer we used to gauge the health of a town's economy was to count the number of boarded-up shops on the main street or in the town square. In 13 communities we visited, more than one fourth of storefronts were either boarded up or permanently padlocked. In three towns, no business community whatsoever was left. In one dilapidated town, a young newspaper publisher, working alone on a Macintosh in a shabby office, lamented to us that this very edition would be the final issue. He told us, "The last grocery store in town just closed last week, and all my advertising has faded into thin air."

All but four communities we toured had faced serious economic decline; three had taken advantage of their natural beauty and recreational potential, while one had benefited from being next door to a large air force base. Even in vacation spots or near military establishments, however, the face of the small community was changing. Even the rather well-off places faced a changing school population and a diminishing sense of community support for the academic life. There was an increasing unskilled work force arriving in small communities to serve the tourists, and a rising population of seniors going there to retire. Neither group was particularly enthusiastic about supporting academic life in the schools.

## THE CHANGING MEMBERSHIP OF SCHOOL BOARDS

As the social characteristics of people served by small districts changed, so also did the compositions of their boards. Whereas school board members used to be known as the "pillars of the community" and were economically secure, on tour we found that many of them had moved away. Many school board members in small communities today are working two or three part-time jobs just to survive. Many large landowners and professionals have moved west and south to the cities and the suburbs of the Sunbelt.

The board members we interviewed were 5 women and 23 men; their occupations included housewife, retiree, self-employed small business owner, farmer, private day-care operator, forestry company employee, highway worker, telephone company mechanic, and dentist. Compared with national statistics, our sample was more male and had fewer people from business and industry, but, from what we understood to be happening in small districts, particularly those in rural areas, our sample was not unusual. In 1989, for example, almost 50% of board members in South Dakota were entrepreneurial farmers and ranchers, and less than 12% were professionals. In the rural regions of Kansas, 50% of board members were farmers and 18% were professionals.

It might be, of course, that an unusually high number of small communities in our sample were suffering from serious economic problems and that the declining interest we found, among professionals and business people, in serving on the board was atypical for the rest of the nation. Still, the repeated pattern of declining interest in working on school boards, among the towns' so-called pillars, was pervasive around the entire route of our tour. We found it, in fact, in 15 of the 25 districts. For example, a retired superintendent in Wisconsin told us, "Thirty years ago, when I became superintendent, the boards had many more professional people. They were made up of doctors, lawyers, dentists, and bankers. As I see things today, it is really hard to get professionals and business leaders to run for school board." An experienced superintendent in Arizona said, "We now have a devil of a time trying to get people with some higher education to run for board positions."

Several teachers told us about their board members' lack of formal education and low commitment to the academic side of school. They used words like, "unintelligent," "anti-intellectual," and even "stupid" to describe particular board members. In one Montana district, five teachers joked sardonically about a graduating senior at the local high school who had difficulty reading. "He'll probably run for the school board next year and become one of our bosses," one of them joked, and the others smiled and nodded in agreement. That wisecrack, although extreme in sarcasm, reflected the disdainful feelings that about 60% of the teachers we interviewed carried about certain board members in their districts. Indeed, we found bitter estrangement between board members and teachers in 10 of the districts.

Superintendents told us that the few professional or business leaders who had stuck it out in economically depressed communities typically refused to run for the board. Small business owners too, with their profits evaporating, considered it too risky to make controversial, public decisions and therefore declined to volunteer for the board. A superintendent in Texas told us, "People say, I can't be bothered; it's too much of a hassle." Another Texas-based superintendent said, "People, good people, say that they can't risk running for the board. The school board has become so political in this district that business people are afraid of losing customers if they take a controversial stand." In a small district in rural Illinois, we interviewed a dentist, one of only two professionals in our board sample, who chose to practice in a small community because he wanted to live there but who actually lost patients because of his vote on a controversial educational issue. Even as we chatted with him,

he was having second thoughts about the wisdom of his serving on
the board.


## BUREAUCRATS VERSUS ENTREPRENEURS

Our travel plan included attending a service at a prominent church
in each community on the day before we started the interviewing.
On tour, we actually attended 12 Catholic or Protestant churches,
choosing to be present at the church with highest membership in that
community. We heeded that guideline everywhere except in Louisiana, where we unexpectedly drove by a small Protestant church in
the country at 11:00 one Sunday morning. Only 15 parishioners were
present; we were immediately invited to become members of that
congregation. Everywhere else, we were more anonymous.

After a church service in a Montana community, we overheard five
parishioners talking about a bitterly contested teachers' strike of a
few years before. The strike apparently was the crowning blow to
what had been a growing estrangement between the teachers and the
board. We learned the next afternoon from the local newspaper editor
that the teachers had struck because of complaints that their insurance and retirement benefits were insufficient. For their part, the
board members, who were locally employed in a depressed economy,
faced difficult times themselves, so they were not particularly sym-
pathetic with the teachers' demands. In our interviews with three
board members, we confirmed a few days later that, except for a
single board member who worked for a forestry-oriented corporation, no board member for quite a few years had had the advantage
of any institutionalized plan for retirement or insurance. It was not
surprising, under those social conditions, that there had been an
increasing rift between teachers and board members in their expectations about publicly financed benefits.

In the majority of the districts we visited, the public school
educators were the only bureaucratic employees in a downwardly
spiraling entrepreneurial economy. As Miller and Swanson (1958)
showed more than 30 years ago, employees of bureaucracies, such

as schoolteachers and hospital nurses, typically have different life and work orientations than those who are self-employed or running a small business, such as carpenters, shop owners, or barbers. Whereas bureaucratic employees expect security, predictability, and consistency in their jobs, the entrepreneurs must take initiative and risks to maintain an adequate income. People working in large bureaucracies must adapt to the social complexities of organizational life; they accept the interpersonal tensions at the workplace in exchange for a reasonable and predictable income. Entrepreneurs, in contrast, mostly work alone or in very small groups; they accept long hours and the risks of a low income in exchange for independence and the distant hope of making it big.

Like many middle- and working-class employees of the bureaucracies in our cities and suburbs, small-district educators think frequently about their insurance and retirement benefits. The entrepreneurs of small communities, conversely, must use business acumen to plan carefully for "rainy days." Compared with their bureaucratic counterparts, the entrepreneurs' financial security is more precarious, and their planning for the distant future, when they have time to do it, more sinuate. We surmise that many small-town entrepreneurs would have difficulty visualizing a retirement of travel and leisure. It is not surprising therefore that teachers and board members in small districts, at times, do not understand one another.

## The Fear of Consolidation

Appropriate accompaniments to the wet weather we encountered were the ominous clouds of district consolidation we found hanging over the heads of board members in small districts. All 28 board members we met, in one way or another, told us that consolidation was the most troubling issue they might have to face. Economic depression, the loss of jobs, and the changing demographic character of small communities had created still another threat to these harassed small-district boards: the pressures for consolidation from the state department of education. We listened to board member after board member tell us about the inevitable consequence of district consolidation: *the loss of community identity.* A board member in Minnesota put it succinctly, "If the district goes, the community dies." In Arizona, a board member told us, "Yes, people here might go to the school for entertainment, but underneath it all is the fact that the school is our primary source of community identity."

Although, in seven of the states we traveled, the legislatures were establishing incentives for small districts to consolidate with one another, no board we visited faced immediate consolidation. There were, however, five boards who had made unpopular decisions to close particular schools. Also, six of the districts had been consolidated in some way in the 1980s. One community in Missouri welcomed district office visitors with a hand-painted sign listing 26 tiny districts that had been drawn into consolidation. We found even many years after consolidation that some animosity between people in the region still existed over the consolidation. In Texas, we visited the Harmony School District. The only public buildings in Harmony were the schools. Since our visit there, we have learned of other districts named Harmony in other states, and their stories seem similar. Several small districts had consolidated, but the people in the several communities could not agree on where to place the schools, so they chose a neutral site, between towns but equally inconvenient to everyone, and established the fantasy community of Harmony in the middle of a large pasture.


## ADAPTABLE COMMUNICATION:
## THE BURDEN OF BOARD MEMBERS


The districts we visited reminded us of glass fishbowls. At the church, the grocery, the restaurant, or in the town square, we would meet people who themselves were either employed by the district or a relative or close friend of a school employee. It was not unusual for a middle school secretary to be married to, or to be the cousin of, a high school teacher, or for an elementary teacher to be married to the middle school principal or to the superintendent. People who live within such tightly interwoven communication channels learn, sometimes the hard way, to heed the aphorism: They who dwell in glass houses should not throw stones.

A brand-new high school math teacher in Arizona told us, "As a newcomer in this district, you learn quickly not to gossip. For all you know, you're talking to someone's sister or uncle." An experienced elementary principal in Texas said, "You have to be very careful here in what you say about others, because it will get back to the person you've been talking about." A board member in Montana admitted, "Frankly I avoid saying anything bad or good about district employees, even to my closest friends and my husband. I've been burned once, and I don't want it to happen again." Board members, administrators, and teachers alike warned us about the dangers to them of their "bad-mouthing" district employees.

In one small district, the school secretaries at the two elementary schools were married to two of the districts' secondary principals; the superintendent's niece, a fourth-grade teacher, was married to the high school baseball coach, whose uncle was on the school board. In another district, the chief custodian's father and grandfather had been the previous two chief custodians for the district. Indeed, he had been born in a cabin on the school grounds. Many of his brothers and sisters, who lived in the community, had attended the local schools, and their children were attending the same schools today.

We wondered if the tightly interwoven kinship networks of small districts would facilitate open communication and accurate exchange of information or whether they might, instead, help to increase the number of false rumors and colorful inaccuracies that would flow from person to person, thereby leading to the illusion that accurate communication about important matters had occurred. The latter seemed to prevail over the former in our experience. From our interviews and observations, we concluded that board members, administrators, and teachers who were relatives frequently were miscommunicating. Many did not realize how much they were misreading one another's messages, however, because many apparently believed that, because they knew one another so well, they must be communicating accurately. Our impression was that the intertwined kinship networks of small districts often served to block clear and accurate communication and, moreover, that the omnipresence of relatives perversely gave people permission to send tactless messages and to tune out critical input.

One board we studied got itself into a peck of trouble, a few years back, with its constituents, because board members dealt only with their relatives about legal, financial, and real estate matters. It seems that building a new high school had been on the board's agenda for a few years, but the citizens could not reach agreement on a site, nor would they consent to paying for it. Then, a lawyer-cousin of one board member told the board that, by way of a technicality in the law, the board could buy land for a new school site without a vote of the people. A banker-brother of another board member arranged the financing, and an uncle of a third board member persuaded the board to buy land he wished to sell. Community residents became furious when the board voted to buy that land without consent of the people. Although the board did purchase the site, the ground had not been broken yet for the new high school. The board's strategy had backfired; now the townspeople would not approve the bond issue to erect the building. The local newspaper editor told us, "The whole deal smelled pretty bad to the people around here." He laughed and went on, "The irony is that the site is just downwind from the largest hog farm in the county. If we build the new high school there, we'll be smelling how bad that deal was every Friday night at our football games for the rest of our lives."

In another district, cousins, nephews, and nieces of board members were teaching in the district. A few of them who taught in the high school, discontented with their principal, complained privately to their relatives on the board about him. The superintendent's secretary kept the board minutes and usually was present when the board held closed sessions. Along with her husband, a shopkeeper, the secretary regularly played cards with the high school principal and his wife. They had been friends for years. During a break at one of the board meetings, she overheard board members sharing information about the teachers' complaints and subsequently warned the principal that some teachers in his school were "out to get him." The superintendent decided to ignore the complaints and did not confer with the principal about them. The principal stopped holding faculty meetings, announcing to the teachers that, for the rest of the year, he would deal with them one-on-one. He stopped talking altogether with the complainants. We left the district not knowing whether the complaints ever were resolved, but we surmised that communication in the district would very likely worsen before it would improve.

To cope with the troublesome pitfalls of kinship networks, small-district board members will have to develop skill in adaptable communication, both in receiving and in sending messages. They must learn how to listen carefully to a variety of people, not only to their relatives, before reaching conclusions, and how to adjust their verbal communications to be responsive to different audiences. A quality educational environment in small districts with limited economic resources requires adaptable communication among the board, citizens, administrators, teachers, and students. Like the North Dakota board we observed, board members of small communities must make a conscientious effort to communicate openly with their various constituencies. They need to listen openly and respond fairly to community members, administrators, teachers, and students.

## EXEMPLARY PRACTICES IN BOARD WORK

Even in the face of trying economic circumstances, changing populations, the threatening clouds of consolidation, and the dysfunctional consequences of tightly interconnected kinship networks, some of the school boards we studied were acting creatively and effectively. In particular, we found five boards that seemed to be coping successfully with the arduous challenges by initiating innovative forms of communication and collaboration in their communities. Two have already been described in Chapter 5. There, we discussed how Ray Pugh and his board in rural Missouri had established what they called the TAB to surface problems, share information, and make recommendations. We also described how a board in Mississippi had had the wisdom to underwrite a carefully executed collaborative planning process to desegregate the high school. Here, we present three other exemplary practices to demonstrate further what school boards might do in small districts to forge links to parents and community.

## *Parent Action for Superior Schools (PASS)*

In most of the 25 small districts we toured, the elementary principals reported high participation in teacher-parent conferences and school open houses. Responses of the secondary principals differed, however, in that parent visits to classrooms and to talk with teachers dropped off precipitously at the middle school or junior high level and dropped off even more at the high school level. Except for the parents' fascination with the allure of high school sports, their active interest in the school's curriculum and instruction decreased as their sons and daughters matured into adolescence. We found, too, that many parents believed that administrators and board members tended to discourage them from participating in the academic life of secondary schools. Indeed, we interviewed seven parents from five different communities who felt intimidated and not welcomed by high school teachers and administrators.

In Montana, a parent group, with the acronym PASS (Parent Action for Superior Schools), had formed to encourage and support parents who wanted to become more engaged in helping the schools at all levels, K-12. We met Josephine Foster, who was a spokesperson for PASS. She herself had graduated from the local high school, and the last of her five children was about to graduate at the time of our interview. She told us, "We wanted to get parents really involved in the education of their youngsters from kindergarten to high school. We put a lot of energy into getting parents of junior high kids involved. That's where there's a dropping off of home involvement."

Foster went on to tell us, "We wanted to help, but the teachers were intimidated by us at first. So we stayed away from the academic side, at first. We did things like safety on buses. We drew lines where the bus kids were supposed to go so they couldn't get in the way of the buses. We put a phone in the middle school for kids to use. Of course, we wanted as much emphasis on academics as athletics, so we put up bulletin boards for academic stars. We developed an academic recognition program. . . . We finally proved ourselves. Our greatest achievement was our PASS tutoring program, in which we've got parent volunteers tutoring kids other than their own. Now, we work closely with the school board. We meet with them every other month, and we get on the agenda of board meetings. We do not take political sides in an election; we just want the schools to be good."

In that Montana-based district, a handful of parents led by Josephine Foster, a parent of five, had taken the initiative to improve the schools. After about two years of effort, the board recognized PASS as an official organization and lauded the parents' efforts at board meetings. Although PASS members at first were considered "suspect" by teachers, for their lack of certified pedagogical experience, PASS members proved their worth to the teachers. By the time of our visit, some three years after their start, PASS activities were appreciated by the board, students, teachers, and administrators.

Our experience in observing the work of PASS proved to us that school boards in small districts can stimulate parent and community initiatives in improving the school's academic program.

## Student Participation in Board Meetings

We found only 1 school board out of 25 that regularly invited high school students to its formal meetings, and that was in Arkansas. There, the board members, administrators, and students all felt satisfied with the students' participation. One board member told us, "I'm impressed with the mature judgment of our student representatives." Another said, "Those students bring a different perspective and that's very important to the board." The superintendent told us, "I'm very pound of our student representatives." And one of the student representatives said, "At first, I was scared, but after while I felt really free to speak my own mind."

Our observations of that district demonstrated to us that student participation in board meetings can be beneficial for at least three reasons: First, student participation on the school board offers the students a memorable educational experience. For, even though board discussions might at times be tedious, they do offer a living experience in community governance and representative democracy. Second, because board members often are not parents of current students in the schools (only 6 of the 28 we interviewed were), and because they have little regular communication with the district's students, student representatives can serve as a ready source of information for board members. And, third, the school board, in striving for adaptable communication skills, should attempt to include as many different voices as possible, to solicit information from and communication with all community groups. The student voice in board discussions can help board members to stay open and receptive to their most important constituency, the students.

## Board-to-Board Relationships

Unless small districts possess special economic advantages, such as a large tourist market or federal impact funds, they often have limited curricular offerings. Although most of the districts we studied were geographically isolated, we were encouraged by the district-to-district and board-to-board cooperation we saw in Wisconsin and Minnesota. There, perhaps inspired by the model of farming cooperatives established in the 1930s and 1940s, school boards and superintendents were purchasing materials collaboratively, sharing specialized classes primarily in vocational and special education, sharing teachers in the sciences and foreign languages, and combining together to amass sufficient numbers for athletic teams, especially in baseball and football.

In Minnesota, county units provided special education resources to small districts. We were particularly impressed in one part of Minnesota where we found cross-district consortia working to upgrade the special education programs in local districts. As was the case in Minnesota, board members can look beyond the boundaries of their own districts to use resources effectively and to improve educational opportunities for all students.

## TARGETS OF CHANGE

There have been few institutions more typically American than the local school board. Even apple pie can be traced to England, and today's small Chevrolet mimics Japanese engineering. But, for more than 200 years, the pervasiveness of school boards has exemplified our American proclivity for grass-roots policies and representative decisions in schooling. For the first 100 years, the school board ran the district; it hired teachers, developed curriculum, supervised instruction, and approved student promotion and graduation. Then, a generation or so after the Civil War, with the appearance of industrialization and urbanization, coupled with the ideology of scientific management, a production prototype for schools arose, which included the role of professional administrator as scientific manager. That administrator, now the superintendent, came to take charge of managerial functions that previously had been carried out by the board.

During the twentieth century, the hegemony of local school boards has continued to deteriorate. There are multiple reasons such as the growing professionalism of school administrators and classroom teachers, and their attendant professional associations, but certainly school consolidation has been one of the most powerful restraints to school board power. School consolidation has meant that, whereas once each board member might have represented 100 or so citizens, now, even in the small districts, board members must each try to represent more than 1,000 citizens. Moreover, with the rise of norm-referenced, psychometric testing of students' intelligence and achievement, and with the growth of a lucrative national textbook market, the capability of lay board members to make informed decisions about local instructional programs and local teaching has faded away.

Now, board members must rely a great deal on the superintendent to give them direction and information. Although, at most board meetings we observed, the board chairperson acted as convener, virtually all agenda items originated with the superintendent. Even the exemplary board we observed in North Dakota relied on two special education teachers and a principal for information about the fourth grader with a learning disability. Indeed, it would appear that, unless board members themselves have advanced training in educational psychology, curriculum, and instruction, they will not be capable of making important educational decisions. Under those circumstances, we might ask: What should become the proper task of the small-district board?

## Task of the Board

Although the primary task of a school board is to set policies that will promote effective programs and practices in the district schools, the small-district board today needs to do more than that. Through communication with teachers and administrators, as in the TAB of the Missouri-based district we already described, the board should prepare a short list of improvement goals for the district to address each year. In fact, the board should decide on a few improvement goals for each school of the district and establish performance objectives for the central administrators, who will be expected to facilitate school improvement. Also, the board should develop its own assessment procedures for tracking whether the administrators and teachers eventually achieve the district's goals and solve the district's problems.

Furthermore, small-district boards should do a couple of other things to enhance their ability to communicate adaptively. Like the Arkansas-based board we observed, they should either invite student representatives from the high school to participate at formal board meetings, or they should create a student advisory group, with which they would have regular and routine communication. Actually, we would prefer a combination of the two. We believe that a small-district board will develop a more objective view of district events if it meets, at least monthly, with a student advisory group and also has three or four students from that group officially in attendance at every board meeting.

Like the Minnesota and Wisconsin boards we saw, small-district boards should attempt to establish communication channels with other boards in their region. Regular contacts with other boards can help surface new ideas for dealing with educational problems and might lead to the sharing of physical resources, teachers, administrators, and curriculum materials. Frequent contacts with board members from outside the district also can help boards guard against the ill effects of gossiping with relatives. Using an objective "sounding board" outside the local district and kinship network can help local boards to see their decisions through the eyes of disinterested, significant others.

## Forging Links to Parents

Parents are concerned about their children's academic performance. They want to understand how the school district works, so that, at home, they can facilitate their children's achievement. Educators believe that, when parents get involved in their children's education, the children's school performance and attitude toward studying improve. Yet, school districts often fail to reach out to parents, and parents, without money or status, are often wary or uncertain about approaching teachers and administrators. We believe that small-district boards should assume the task of forging links between parents and the schools.

It took Josephine Foster and her friends two years to gain official recognition from the board. PASS proved itself in that district and became known in neighboring districts as a positive approach to school improvement. Now, more districts in Montana are experimenting with alternative forms of parent involvement. Some of those districts are using the services of parents as paraprofessionals. Also, Joseph Gomez has introduced the idea of parents as paraprofessionals in his Arizona-based district. According to an edition of *Educational Leadership,* which appeared in October 1989 (Merenda, 1989), just a few months after our tour, partnerships between parents and schools are being formed all over the United States, and parents as paraprofessionals is a key idea in many of them.

Parents as paraprofessionals typically are mothers or seniors who have not been formally trained as teachers but who have a strong interest in helping youngsters. The specific uses of paraprofessionals differ from one small district to another. Generally, they assist with clerical functions (keeping attendance, typing, copying, and computing) or serve as instructional aides. In some districts, parents as instructional aides assist the teacher in the classroom, while, in other districts, parents also take full responsibility for tutoring and coaching specific students. Paraprofessional parents might also assume such functions as managing the library or media center or helping to set up instructional materials, audiovisual aids, and graphics.

In Arizona and New Mexico, the involvement of poor mothers served as a means of part-time employment and bolstered the well-being of their families. As Joseph Gomez told us, "Many chores and functions of our schools can be performed quite well by motivated parents who do not have the full credentials of teachers." And it was our observation that, when record-keeping tasks and instructional-materials development were carried out by parents, the teachers had more time to work directly with the students. Furthermore, the use of parents from the "other side of the tracks" offered increased pluralism in the schools of Arizona and New Mexico. Thus low-income Hispanic and Apache students, who related primarily to white middle-class teachers, were being tutored by Hispanic and Apache adults; while middle-class students, who seldom interacted with minority group citizens, were being tutored by adults from neighborhoods quite different than theirs. As other examples, we observed parents with special hobbies or particular skills being enlisted to volunteer a few hours a month to their local schools.

There can be other ways too that parents might contribute to the mission of the school. In doing our pilot study for this research in the spring of 1988, we came across a small district in Oregon in which some parents were employed by the district to carry out preschool training in their homes. The parents, again mostly mothers, were given training by teachers in developing readiness skills in preschoolers. They visited the homes of the preschool children to meet with the mothers and children together. They suggested activities that the mother could use routinely with the child, such as sorting socks by color, counting the number of people for dinner, separating forks, knives, and spoons, and so on, and provided learning games that the parent and child could play together.

Another concept for parent participation is the community school, which fits the small district like a glove. The school, in this concept, is formally designated by the board as the educational center of the community, where all local citizens can come together as teachers and learners. The district's educational program, in other words, is not only for youngsters but is for people of all ages. Courses covering such diverse topics as the arts, computers, cooking, child care, crafts, first aid, the modern novel, and recreation can be offered at any time of day or night.

The most prominent model for the community school was developed in Flint, Michigan, under the leadership and funding of the Mott Foundation. In one form envisioned in Flint, the community school opened its library doors, cafeteria lines, and classroom desks to people of all backgrounds and ages. In another version in Flint, all community participants were viewed as potential participants. The philosophy was that everyone should be seen as possessing resources and needs and that the function of the school should be to match the resources with the needs. The staff of a community school, in the Flint model, was to have diagnosed learning needs in the community, discovered the community's resources, managed the program, and helped to organize the learning opportunities of all interested participants. We believe that small-district boards should carry out the diagnoses of learning needs and teaching resources but then pass on the responsibilities of program management, organization, and implementation to the superintendent.

If the board takes a strong stand in support of the community school, then small-district schools will have a better chance than they have today of becoming everybody's house. In the ideal community school, all local citizens, regardless of age, occupation, sex, race, and ethnicity, are defined as learners and potential teachers; all have something to offer; and the programs will be based on interests, needs, and available resources. The local people themselves are the school.

Unfortunately, most of the schools in the small districts we visited had not even tried to become community schools. School as a place for students continued to be the norm, and adults went to the schools primarily to be entertained by the students. Real person-to-person communication between students and adults was rare. Even though in a few places some intergenerational communication was occurring, and some parents were acting productively as paraprofessionals, the citizens for the most part did not view the district as an educational community for everyone.

### Forging Links to Community

Board members are *partners* in their advocacy for educational excellence in the schools. Indeed, the concept of educational partners, associates who share a common interest in enhancing student learning, offers a useful way of thinking about a district's effectiveness in making school everybody's house.

We can search for partners at all system levels of a district: Examples are older students tutoring younger students; students cooperating to learn and learning to cooperate; teachers teaming for instruction; seasoned teachers mentoring neophyte teachers; principals convening problem-solving discussions with teachers; superintendents engaging principals in consensus decision making; board members, administrators, and teachers exchanging perceptions about district strengths and weaknesses; and board members working with parent groups for school improvement.

School boards also can extend the concept of educational partners to include cooperation between the district and community organizations, such as businesses, churches, governmental agencies, and service clubs. According to Daniel Merenda (1989), the Executive Director of the National Association of Partners in Education, the most popular partnerships between schools and community organizations are district-business partnerships. In fact, most of the literature on partnerships that we have read has focused on schools collaborating with large corporations, such as Amoco, IBM, and Xerox, or with brokers for clusters of large corporations, such as the Economic Development Council of New York and the National Alliance of Business.

Merenda pointed out that, although the most common type of partnership entails volunteers from large corporations assisting classroom teachers in instruction, several other potent kinds of district-business partnerships have been under way for more than 20 years, such as collaborative pinpointing of needed school reforms, like computer literacy, and then working together to make the reforms happen; bringing corporation and school managers together for mutual assistance on administrative problems in the schools; or infusing teacher preparation programs in math and science with field experiences in industry.

Although Merenda wrote that district-business partnerships are on the rise, and that by 1990 as many as 40% of American schools could have been affected by them, our experiences on the blue highways, along with a literature review of prominent district-business partnerships, indicated that large districts much more than small districts have benefited from them. Furthermore, most district-business partnerships have focused on how the corporation can contribute to the schools, seldom the other way around. The rationale seems to be that corporations will benefit eventually from a competent pool of prospective employees.

We believe that small-district boards, particularly those in economically devastated communities, should attempt to forge links to the community by entering into *two-way partnerships* with local organizations, in which the schools and the organization will benefit immediately. For example, many small districts have a retirement park or nursing home nearby. Students could spend time with senior citizens, reading to them or writing letters for them. Or students could interview a senior about the latter's life and then write an essay about the interview. Seniors could help the students review for a test, give them ideas for a paper, drill them on math facts, spelling, or word definitions, or they might visit the school, if they are able, to observe classes or even to tutor in study halls. Also, small districts usually have a service club in the vicinity, such as the Kiwanis, Lions, or Rotary. The students could find out about the charitable mission of one of those organizations and brainstorm ways in which the students and service club members, by cooperating, could contribute to the community's well-being.

Small-district boards even should consider ways in which the schools could take initiative to contribute to the community's economic vitality. Paul Nachtigal (1991), an expert in rural education, has argued that, to keep schools in rural communities, we will have to become clever about how the school itself might facilitate local economic development. High school students could work with representatives from the local businesses, governmental agencies, and service clubs to come up with innovative ideas for new products or services that might be introduced into the community. Perhaps, through activities similar to those of Junior Achievement, the local chamber of commerce could enlist students to act like entrepreneurs for the community. After all, most of our computer wizards are probably under 30, and it is likely to be the communication revolution of the twenty-first century that will either save or doom our small communities.

## REFERENCES

Merenda, D. (1989). Partners in education: An old tradition renamed. *Educational Leadership, 47*(2), 4-7.

Miller, D., & Swanson, G. (1958). *The changing American parent.* New York: John Wiley.

Nachtigal, P. (1991). Rural grassroots school organizations: Their agendas for education. In A. De Young (Ed.), *Rural education: Issues and practice.* New York: Garland.

Ratner, J. (1939). *Intelligence in the modern world: John Dewey's philosophy.* New York: Modern Library.

# 7

# Restoring the Dream of a United House

## BLUEPRINTS FOR ACTION

The higher one's view of the human potential, the more one
will dislike the schools as they actually exist.

*—Mayer, 1961, p. 426*

One chilly December evening two decades ago, a few months before
our daughter's 7th birthday and our son's 4th, the four of us drove
the streets of Eugene to look at holiday decorations. Magnificent
cedars, firs, pines, and spruce, brightly illuminated with green, red,
and white spotlights, graced the parks, and multicolored cone-shaped
bulbs gave radiant light to the trees, bushes, and roof lines of the
houses. Eugene, all aglow, was a child's delight. Living room drapes
were open to expose colorful household decorations to the outside.
We pointed to the homes of our colleagues: "Look, Julie and Allen,
there's the Abbotts' house, the Carlsons', the Charters'; and look,

there's the Runkels' house." Soon we drove past a school, its windows decked out with white cardboard snowflakes, red paper bells, and sprigs of evergreens and holly tied with green ribbons. Bright-eyed Julie, silent until that moment, exclaimed, "Look, look, there's the school, it's everybody's house!"

Over the years, Julie's delightful utterance has afforded us a poignant metaphor for musing about an American dream—that school could be everybody's house. We traveled 10,000 miles to see whether small districts, more than their metropolitan counterparts, were chasing that dream. Although the districts we visited served as the magnetic gathering places for most citizens in their communities, and while many educators were doing outstanding jobs under difficult circumstances, we seldom saw the sorts of interpersonal collaboration or group synergy that we had hoped to find. Too often, we uncovered a divided and troubled house, in which board members were at odds with educators, administrators were putting off or putting down teachers, teachers were talking down to students, and students' views were not being heard or heeded by teachers, administrators, or board members.

As we toured the countryside, we read again Bellah, Madsen, Sullivan, Swidler, and Tipton (1985), the Lynds (1929), Reisman et al. (1950), and Tocqueville (1945), and we reflected on our own careers as educators. In our reveries, we conceived our dream to be part of the grand historical sweep of the American experience. To paraphrase what the educational historian, Lawrence Cremin (1980), wrote about the birth of the United States: From the beginning of our nation, we have sought to use the schools to create a cohesive and interdependent citizenry, to persuade the youth to choose public over private interests, and to improve our social conditions continually. We realized from reading Cremin and the others that the dream of making school everybody's house was part of the mainsprings of American culture.

Our professional careers have been dedicated to enhancing communication, collaboration, and cooperation in schools. We have sought to make schools more democratic. We have pursued those objectives as students, teachers, administrators, parents, consultants, and scholars. In fact, we have been engaged with public schools since we were 5 years old, never having spent one month since then without doing some formal learning, teaching, or research within schools. During the early elementary years, we were students in small districts. After that, we were either students or educators in only metropolitan districts and large universities. At the time of this writing, we estimated that we had administered, consulted, researched, studied, or taught in more than 300 school districts worldwide.

Although what we experienced in most small districts was discouraging, it did not break our spirit or reduce our commitment to the public schools. We still can visualize the American dream of schools contributing to the public good and social improvement. We also can personally attest to the fact that some schools already are creating the conditions for a cohesive and interdependent community. Much like the Joad family, or like Huck Finn and Jim, we still travel in search of a more humane America. We feel deeply rooted in the American experience; formal schooling has been exceedingly good to us. For us, cultural and personal forces converge on the core belief of optimism in the future, or what Tocqueville saw as the "American faith in progress." We embrace the cultural assumption that schools, more than any other American institution, can make the social order better for more and more people with each succeeding generation and that we will realize that more and more when everyone pulls together.

The divided and troubled houses of America's small districts can be repaired. We are optimistic about that. We met scores of educators, students, parents, and board members who would lend a helping hand to refurbishing their schools and communities. We estimate, overall, that at least 50% of the people we met would agree that restoring the dream of a united house in small districts is desirable, feasible, and timely. We submit the following blueprints for action to help small districts repair and rebuild their divided houses.

## PILASTERS OF CONSTRUCTION

Dreams of a rebuilt house ultimately must be transformed into blueprints. The blueprints of early American architects, such as those of Thomas Jefferson, often called for decorative columns or pilasters to help buttress the superstructure of the roof. Pilasters were slender, rectangular supports or piers with a base, shaft, and capital. In construction, the base of the pilaster mass attached to the foundation, the shaft rose from the floor and engaged the wall, and the capital undergirded the ceiling or roof. We believe that at least three figurative pilasters should be used today in constructing a united school district: *transactional communication, polyarchic influence,* and *respect for the individual.*

## Transactional Communication

The first, transactional communication, is a highly valued procedure in writings about cooperative learning and organization development. According to Schmuck and Runkel (1988), it is a reciprocal exchange of information in which each participant strives to be helpful to the other. Messages are sent in both directions ensuring that mutual feedback will occur. The roles of sender and receiver alternate quickly back and forth, and each strives to listen actively. Moreover, active listening entails attempting to fathom both ideas and feelings, zeroing in on the sender's point of view, and testing understanding by attempting to paraphrase the sender's message. To initiate effective transactional communication, the sender must articulate his or her thoughts and feelings clearly but also be ready to listen carefully to the receiver's response. Both participants should ask each other for a clarification, while trying to read the meaning of the other's gestures. Transactional communication is a necessary ingredient for I-Thou transactions.

## Polyarchic Influence

The second, polyarchic influence, has been a favorite concept among organizational theorists. In classic research performed at the University of Michigan, Likert (1961) and Tannenbaum (1968) demonstrated that it is feasible for genuine power to be wielded at every hierarchical level in a business, social agency, or school. They used the words *polyarchic influence* to refer to organizational structures in which three or more subgroups, such as the board, administrators, teachers, and students, were sharing power over important organizational decisions. In their field experiments and observational studies, they showed that organizations with polyarchic influence structures were more effective than those with top-down or anarchic structures in accomplishing their goals.

Our advocacy for a wider distribution of power than we found in districts on the blue highways is based not only on that research but also on the moral principle that it is just for schools to be governed by the people who live in them and are affected by them. Small districts, in particular, should be models of community cohesiveness and interdependence. They should put public interests high on their agendas and strive to improve the social conditions of their communities.

To paraphrase the political scientist Robert Dahl's (1970) "Principle of Affected Interests": The teachers or students who are affected by the decision of an administration should have the right to participate, in some way, in that decision. And, according to Tannenbaum, increased influence at the lower echelons need not reduce the control of administrators higher up. Indeed, polyarchic influence, like love, tends to be reciprocal and cumulative across hierarchical levels, making it easier for the organizational participants to pull together toward common goals. New polyarchic influence structures also should be created in small districts to augment I-Thou exchanges between individuals at different status levels.

## Respect for the Individual

The third, respect for the individual, has been a core American value since the birth of the culture. When we were a brand-new nation, and pioneers were forced to adapt to a variety of harsh, environmental challenges, the values of individualism, familial autonomy, hard work, and self-control were mostly utilitarian. Reisman et al. (1950) described the typical character type of early America as inner directed. They painted the portrait of a steadfast and individuated people for whom the opinions of others were less important than their own beliefs about right and wrong. An extreme example of the flaw of the inner-directed character occurred during the fateful trip of the Donner party over the Sierra Nevada mountains. In the face of death, members maintained family autonomy and interpersonal competition, even though, with more community collaboration and between-family sharing, many of the party probably would have survived. Bellah et al. (1985) described a tension in America today between the value of truculent individualism, "the me generation," on the one hand, and a pressing requirement for cooperation, collaboration, and community, on the other hand.

As we contemplated the study by Bellah et al. and visited with the people of America's small districts, we recognized the need to redefine the concept of individualism for the twenty-first century. Even though contemporary thought about respect for individuals represents a mainspring of American culture, it must take on a different core meaning today. Respect for the individual today must emphasize respect for individuals, regardless of their class, ethnicity, gender, handicap, race, religion, or social status. It is respect for whole persons, regardless of their social category, that we must go after as well as a striving for more authentic I-Thou exchanges between individuals who are quite different from one another.

The sort of communication and cooperation required for living up to the new value of respect for whole persons will be difficult to realize. We understand, as educators ourselves, that it will be emotionally taxing for teachers to interact as whole persons with students and for administrators to strive for I-Thou exchanges with teachers. Even in small districts, where tininess makes it feasible to realize the value of respect for whole persons, interpersonal closeness, openness, and support will still present a herculean task.

Too many of the small districts we observed, however, either neglected or ignored the importance of personal relationships in teaching, learning, and administering. Too many schools were characterized by superficial and distant relationships, covert hostility and cynicism, and too little mutual concern or respect among administrators, teachers, and students. We concluded that, when administrators and teachers paid too little attention to students, as whole persons, the academic objectives of cognitive and skill development were hindered, and, when administrators and teachers didn't see one another as whole persons, their ability to solve academic problems together was hindered.

The figurative pilasters in the restoration of the American dream of a united school district must be constituted of respect for the individual, transactional communication, and polyarchic influence. Respect for the individual is at the pilaster's base and forms the foundation of the academic program. Transactional communication ranges up and down the pilaster's shaft and brings common understandings to the school's participants. Polyarchic influence mounts the pilaster at its most ornate section, the capital, and serves as a superstructure fostering collaborative relationships among the board, administrators, teachers, students, and community. The three parts of the pilaster combine to support more whole-person relationships and I-Thou exchanges and to nurture growth toward a more united district. The blueprints of this restoration also include some specific actions of boards, superintendents, principals, teachers, and students.

## EVERYBODY'S PART IN DISTRICT REBUILDING

For decades, American schools have been badgered in the press because of students' low test scores in language and math as well as their weak preparation in science. More recently, public schools have come under fire because they have failed to prepare America's teenagers adequately in job-related social skills such as collaborative planning, effective teamwork, and cooperative decision making. Indeed, a national commission on our teenagers and future jobs convened by the labor secretary in 1991 recommended that schools, businesses, and communities pull together to make our young people's skills for working competently with others as much a part of their education as reading, writing, math, and science. We concur with that stand but also believe strongly that collaboration, teamwork, and cooperation must occur more often on school boards, between the school and its community, and among administrators and teachers before it will firmly take hold in classrooms. It will take concerted collaboration on everybody's part to rebuild our school districts into a united house, where collaboration, teamwork, and cooperation are a regular and routine way of life.

## The Board's Part

Boards must take the initiative to prepare a list of district improvement goals each year. The list should be organized with three categories of goals: respect for the individual, transactional communication between district subgroups, and polyarchic influence across hierarchical levels. The board should also consider the following actions:

1. The board should create a student advisory group, with which it has regular and routine communication, and invite student representatives from the group to participate in formal board meetings.
2. The board should create a formal advisory group, made up of administrators, community representatives, parents, and teachers, to bring up districtwide problems and to brainstorm potential solutions.
3. The board should seek regular contacts with other boards in the region to help surface new ideas for dealing with academic problems and to test the feasibility of sharing educational resources.
4. The board should forge links with parents and the community. It should consider alternative ways of soliciting parent involvement in the schools, including employment of parents as paraprofessionals as well as parents being teachers and learners in a community school. It also should review how the businesses of the community could contribute to academic life and how academic course work could contribute to the economic development of the community.

## The Superintendent's Part

Superintendents must trumpet, through speeches, one-to-one interactions, memos, and articles in the local newspaper, the critical importance of respect for the individual, transactional communication, and polyarchic influence for the well-being of the district, the community, and the nation. The superintendent should also consider the following actions:

1. Superintendents should present a collaborative leadership model to their principals by striving to solve problems cooperatively and making decisions consensually.
2. Superintendents should solicit feedback about their own helpful or unhelpful role behaviors from the principals; next, encourage debriefing discussions with the principals about the effective and ineffective aspects of the administrative team; and then lead the administrative team in discussions about the strengths and shortcomings of the district's schools.
3. Superintendents should hold both formal and informal meetings with students so that students' ideas and feelings can influence district procedures for selecting new teachers and assessing effective teaching. Also, superintendents should see to it that students' concerns appear on the agendas of administrative team meetings.
4. Superintendents should declare publicly and frequently how very important teachers are to the success of the district. Also, they should model that belief behaviorally by visiting every teacher's classroom for at least 30 minutes once a year.
5. Superintendents should deliberately set out to be the educational leaders of their communities. They should appear at a variety of community meetings to solicit psychological support for lifelong education and to articulate the theme that school is the education center for everyone in the community, regardless of age.

## The Principal's Part

Of all small-district educators, principals are positioned best in the district structure to encourage I-Thou transactions and to foster group cohesiveness and esprit de corps in the school. As the primary authority figure, the principal should show respect for individuals by gathering personal information about every teacher and student and articulating their strengths to each of them in one-to-one interaction. The principal should model transactional communication, by listening empathically to each individual and responding with friendly and supportive words, as well as polyarchic influence, by bringing together formal groups of teachers and students for advice, to solve problems, and to make decisions. The principal also should consider the following actions:

1. Principals should be visible in the classrooms, hallways, lunchroom, and school grounds to talk informally with teachers and students about personal and professional matters.
2. Principals should also recognize the power of formal meetings and strive to make them effective by assiduously attending to agenda preparation, the roles of convener and recorder, the use of communication skills, and meeting debriefing.
3. Principals should establish link-pin and matrix organizational structures so that all students and teachers have at least the possibility of communicating and influencing other teachers and the principal.
4. Principals should strive to upgrade teaching and learning in the school by taking the four roles, at appropriate times, of action researcher, social architect, staff developer, and political strategist.

## The Teacher's Part

Teachers can make or break efforts to bring a sense of unity to the small district; however, when administrators show respect for teachers, foster transactional communication with them, and allow for teachers to influence district decision making, then most teachers will enthusiastically try to establish more collaboration, cooperation, and community in the school. The teacher should consider the following actions:

1. Teachers should initiate some new forms of collegial collaboration, such as peer sharing, coaching, and consultation.

2. Teachers should try to reduce student boredom with academic learning by exploring a greater variety of activity structures in the classroom than they typically use today.
3. Teachers should learn how to integrate cooperative learning appropriately into their instructional strategies.
4. Teachers should deliberately design ways in which the academic culture, so typical of their orientation, can be supplemented with both personal and application cultures.

## The Student's Part

Compared with adult professionals, students are most affected by the lack of unity and cohesiveness in the district. It should not be surprising that our youth are not learning how to plan collaboratively, to work in teams effectively, or to make decisions cooperatively. They see too few adults who are modeling such behaviors. Ultimately, students must become the focus of the educators' attempts to show respect for the individual, implement transactional communication, and construct formal structures to foster polyarchic influence. Small-district educators should help students to take the following actions:

1. Students should be thought of as organizational participants in the school, not as the products of the school, and be granted more formal power to influence how the school operates.
2. Students should be asked for their perceptions of good and bad teaching; they should be encouraged to participate in the selection of new teachers and in the assessment of current teaching in the school.
3. Students should be encouraged to tackle tasks on the student council that go beyond the entertainment function of the school. They should also be working on ways to improve curriculum and instruction in the school and to nurture the organizational development of administrators, teachers, and students.
4. Students should be encouraged to dream up and try out innovative ways of contributing to community development.

*    *    *

Many small districts have big problems. They lack mutual understanding, collaboration, and cooperation between administrators and teachers. They lack norms and procedures that foster listening to students. They lack a sense of everyone pulling together. To restore the dream of a united house, they will have to look within themselves. Each small district will have to recognize its own special problems first. Then, although the rebuilding will require everyone's participation, the spark for change will be ignited by one board member, administrator, or teacher who still hopes that school can be everybody's house.

## REFERENCES

Bellah, R. N., Madsen, R., Sullivan, W., Swidler, A., & Tipton, S. (1985). *Habits of the heart.* New York: Harper & Row.

Cremin, L. (1980). *American education: The national experience, 1783-1876.* New York: Harper & Row.

Dahl, R. (1970). *After the revolution.* New Haven, CT: Yale University Press.

Likert, R. (1961). *Patterns of management.* New York: McGraw-Hill.

Lynd, R., & Lynd, H. M. (1929). *Middletown: A study of contemporary American culture.* New York: Harcourt Brace.

Mayer, M. (1961). *The schools.* New York: Harper.

Reisman, D., with N. Glazer and R. Denny. (1950). *The lonely crowd: A study of the changing American character.* New Haven, CT: Yale University Press.

Schmuck, R., & Runkel, P. (1988). *The handbook of organization development in schools.* Prospect Heights, IL: Waveland.

Tannenbaum, A. (1968). *Control in organizations.* New York: McGraw-Hill.

Tocqueville, A. de (1945). *Democracy in America.* New York: Knopf.

# Index